Phenomenal

BFF Publishing House is a Limited Liability Corporation dedicated wholly to the appreciation and publication of books for children and adults for the advancement of diversification in literature.

For more information on publishing contact:

Antionette Mutcherson at

bff@bffpublishinghouse.com

Website: bffpublishinghouse.com

Published in the United States by

BFF Publishing House

Atlanta, Georgia First Edition, 2023

ISBN: 979-8-9890667-0-4

Contents

Chapter 1

RAQSTAR LIFESTYLE:
I WILL MAKE IT

Dedicated to the wisdom of my ancestors Arzella, Shawn, Karen, DeLois, Ruth, and Alicia. Thank you for protecting me. Asé.

In Tune

On a crisp Friday morning in Charlotte, North Carolina, a baby chose to enter this realm. Though she was scheduled to rest in her mother's womb until April, the letters on the 1999 calendar noted January as the current month. The next day, a Saturday, was scheduled to be her only brother's seventh birthday. Certainly, her family was concerned about planning for a celebratory weekend—until, in a truly radical fashion, the baby decided that *this* would be the day she came into the world. On that fateful Friday morning, her mother's water broke, and the pair was suddenly rushed to the hospital.

Unrecognizable by her doctor due to total-body swelling from high blood pressure, her mother was immediately scheduled for an emergency C-section. Once removed, the baby cried out into the world with reckless abandon. Her heart beat to a steady rhythm, and her soul stirred in preparation for her new lived experience. Her brother held her closely and felt as though this newborn reminded him of an angel.

At three pounds and two point four ounces, that tiny baby was truly a wonder. She was kept in the hospital for two weeks before being connected with her family. She was named after an international icon, Jo Raquel Tejada, a.k.a. Raquel Welch. That baby was me.

While I have no recollection of my life from ages zero to three, when I look back at pictures of myself as a baby with gray eyes, I appear to be radiant and content. There are photos of my mom playing with a Tweety Bird stuffed animal with me, showing me that she was eager to serve as a present figure in my life.

When I got older, my mother told me that when we would enter grocery stores, kind strangers would hand her cash as a compliment. She also reflected on moments when she was a real estate agent, beaming with pride at her memories of bringing me to house showings and people consistently making a deal to close on the home. She would always tell me, "You are a miracle and a masterpiece."

At the tender age of three, I was preyed upon by a woman working as an employee of the daycare I frequented. Right before the day ended, as children scurried to clean up and prepare for parent pick-up, she capitalized on the frenzy and would lure me into the bathroom. I am unsure of how often I was molested, but it did happen multiple times. I had no knowledge of what rape was or what was happening to me. Due to a series of compounded trauma throughout my lived experience, these memories were erased from my mind until I began experiencing nightmares at the age of thirteen. I told no one.

In 2003, less than two weeks after my fourth birthday, my mother received a phone call detailing the fact that her oldest sister suddenly passed away. I remember bringing her my stuffed animals to attempt to console her as she became overwhelmed with tears. The grief of suddenly losing my aunt would be a pain that my mother carried for the rest of her life. That same year, perhaps due to wanting to escape from the trauma she endured in her hometown, she moved me and my brother to Georgia with a shattered heart.

Set List

Hillview Lane

One of my earliest memories is of a yellow house on Hillview Lane in Douglasville, Georgia. At this time, I was in the third grade. Nothing mattered more to me than going to school, playing alongside my brother, and enjoying my mother's food for supper. Back then, I did not realize how fortunate I was to have a brother who, although he is seven years older than me, would make funny faces and ascribe personalities to my dolls and stuffed animals in a game we called "*Toy Life*." To have an older brother who would come home from school and teach me what I naively referred to as "three-number math," a.k.a. equations like "four hundred and thirty-five plus five hundred and sixty-four equals nine hundred and ninety-nine."

To have a mother who, after hours of work, would come home to prepare my favorite meal: spaghetti with warm, decadent garlic bread from my favorite brand, *New York Bakery*. She affectionately gifted me with the nicknames "Raq 'n' Roll" and "RaqStar." She referred to herself, me, and my brother as CVT, Inc. to unite us due to all of us having different last names.

She dressed stylishly and smelled of sweet vanilla perfume. She had an affinity for butterflies and found them captivating and beautiful. In her free time, we would listen to CDs in her car and jam out to rap and rhythm and blues music. Even from a young age, I witnessed her work very hard, yet she still remained radiant and beautiful while making time for fun.

I remember my dad being present every now and then. When he was around, I always felt pure joy because I had everyone I loved under the same roof. I reveled in the positivity that came when Mom, Dad, Brother, and I were together. My mom explained to me that my dad drove trucks for Swift Transportation.

Sure enough, time would pass, and Dad would receive a new assignment and have to leave again. If my mom's car happened to pass an eighteen-wheeler with *SWIFT* written in big, chunky blue lettering, I peered into the driver's window, hoping to see a familiar face. I didn't realize it, but a long time passed before I realized that Dad hadn't returned for a while. It would take me nine years to understand what the word *relapse* entailed.

I came home from school, kicked off my shoes, tossed my coat, and realized that it was dark in the house. I went over to a light switch. *Flip up, flip down, flip up . . . flip down, flipup, flipdown, flipup.* To no avail, the lightbulbs weren't working. *What is happening? I mean, I thought this is how electricity works.* I decided to open up a workbook and practice my handwriting. Maybe when Mom and Brother got home, I would get another three-number math lesson . . . I was starting to enjoy the challenge. Shadows cascaded across the living room as the sun left the sky.

I was playing with my toys when my mom and brother returned with plastic bags from Walmart. *OooOOO! They went shopping!* I don't really know what I was expecting, but it certainly wasn't a flashlight, batteries, and two things that my mom explained were portable lamps. I thought the lamps were cute! One was shaped like a soccer ball, and the other was shaped like a basketball. When you put two AA batteries inside each of them and pressed the top, vibrant hues emanated from them. Feeling pleased with a new object and happy to have a bit of light in the home, I asked my brother if he wanted to teach me three-number math.

"Not today," he sullenly replied.

It was pretty dark out, and I had school the next day, so I decided to get ready for bed. With my soccer ball portable lamp on the counter, confusion overtook me as I started the shower. I usually kept the shower handle right between the blue and red lines, but on this day, I cranked the handle until it was in the red on the farthest side. *Whew! What is happening?! The water is sooooo chilly!*

That school was my main priority. In third grade, Ms. Boot was my homeroom teacher, and the first subject of the day was always math. I always finished my work early. Maybe it was because of those math lessons my brother gave me after school. I never invited friends over, and I did not play any recreational sports, so going to school and seeing all my pals excited me. In my eyes, I just wanted to talk to my classmates and see how they were doing as people. I didn't understand why Ms. Boot always moved my desk and turned it toward the wall.

At home, the lights still did not shine. Now, Mom would be gone for really long hours, too. Looking back, my brother really helped me hold on to my innocence. He continued to play with toys alongside me. We read books, drew pictures, and reveled in our imaginations. I had no idea the gravity of our situation.

Duralee Lane

One day after school, instead of returning to the yellow house, we pulled into a parking lot. There was a sign that read *Crown Inn*, and it featured a gold crown blanketed in a purple background. I had never been on vacation, but I genuinely wondered if that's what we were doing. Oh, how young I was to think that we were vacationing in the same town we lived in. I'm going to be honest: I don't remember much from this time in my life.

I was still going to school, but Mom started getting mad at me because I would have to bring her notes from my teacher. When she wasn't with us at home—whoops, I mean at the hotel—I snuck and read the paper. There, in full capital letters, it read: RAQUEL TALKS TOO MUCH AND IS A DISTRACTION TO HER PEERS. I RECOMMEND HER REMOVAL FROM THE GIFTED PROGRAM. *Huh? Did Ms. Boot write this? Man, bump this. I HATE math!*

My memories of this time in my life are a bit fragmented. One moment that I remember quite vividly is a day when my brother and I were playing together in the room. We were most likely jumping from each bed and running around. When my brother got tired, he called off our rambunctious playtime, and he asked me to help him start remaking the beds. As he gathered the flat, white bed sheet off the floor, I initiated a game of tug-of-war. He asked me multiple times to get off of the sheet, and in defiance, I refused. I remember my brother firmly yelling, *"GET OFF!"* and with one swift yank, I collapsed to the floor. My foot slipped on the slick sheet, and the top right of my head cracked into the foot of the metal bed frame.

To both of our horror, blood flowed uncontrollably out of my new wound. In a flash, my mother came back to the room. She saw the deep gash, miraculously located about an inch away from my temple, and immediately began praying over me. She prayed that the bleeding would stop, that I would be able to make a full recovery. While she consoled me with her prayers, she placed a hand on the spot where I was injured. Her hand began to feel scorching hot as she asked God to be an ever-present help in our time of trouble. She called God out on the promises listed in the Bible.

Before I realized, the bleeding stopped, and I was able to get some rest. This is the first time I realized the power of prayer and my mother's healing hands. As an adult, the impact of the wound is barely visible. I look back on this time in awe at my mother's ability to work through shock and fear. All I have from that moment is this memory rather than a gnarly scar.

I jolted from my sleep as tall people in black uniforms burst through the door. I remember bright flashlights and shiny badges and scary belts with lots of tools on them. I remember my brother and I being taken away. Everything is blank. Though I do not remember living through this, I later found out that a custody battle took place between different extended family members to decide who would house me and my brother.

Queensdale Drive

No Mom. No Dad. *I really miss them.* Now, my brother and I lived with my father's sister and her husband, whom I was familiar with. I knew there was a history of conflict between the two of them and my mom, so I didn't really understand why we were living with them.

I witnessed my brother undergo vicious physical abuse at the hands of my father and the person I was instructed to refer to as my uncle. I was so angry. My brother was not only my best friend but also the most intelligent person I ever knew. *Why is he punching my brother? Why won't they leave him alone?* I was paralyzed by *fear*. I heard my brother's screams. I didn't know what to do about them.

One day, my brother found a way to contact the police and told them what was going on in the home. Sure enough, the tall people in black uniforms came back. I was instructed to stay inside, but peeking through my bedroom blinds, I saw red and blue lights. I saw my dad's sister talking to the police, but my brother was not there in the yard with them.

Later, a neighbor told me that she saw the police handcuff my brother and put him in the back of the car. I guess I didn't really realize that there were witnesses to what was going on in my life. I didn't even get a chance to say goodbye to my best friend before he was sent to foster care. No Mom. No Dad. No Brother.

I remember my dad's sister telling me that my mom was in the hospital with pneumonia. I had no idea what pneumonia was, but it scared me to hear the word *hospital*. At this time, I hadn't seen my mom in two years. I naturally asked if I could see my mom, and when I was told "no," I genuinely felt *despair*. She also explained to me that the man who had been present in my life since I was born was not my biological father; my mother had mentioned this to me in the past. In a sick way, I began to understand that this so-called caregiver was isolating me from every person I ever loved.

School became my saving grace. I was in the fourth grade, and I found that my father's sister and her husband left me alone if I continued to bring home exceptional grades as my mother encouraged me. I spent most of my time reading the Merriam-Webster dictionary. I learned how to regurgitate information presented by the teachers, I knew how to study, thanks to my brother, and I learned to produce a quality of work that would continue giving me straight A's. After school, I would find solace in exploring the forest behind their home, and I established reverence for nature. Grounding myself amongst the trees imbued me with lessons of openness, peace, and endurance.

My caregivers also started talking to me about music lessons to give me something to do on the weekends. *OooOOO! That's so cool. I would love to play the guitar!* I told my father's sister of my vision for myself, to which she hastily replied, "That's for boys. It gives you calluses, and it will make your hands ugly." One evening, her husband came home with a slender black case. He marched to the closet in my room, placed it on the top shelf, and sneered as he instructed me not to touch it. *Well, that was smart of him. I can't reach up there, anyway.*

What I mainly remember from this time in my life is undergoing weekly flute lessons with a white woman with very long, gray tresses. I liked her a lot and looked forward to trailing up her driveway, situated upon a long hill, in preparation for my lessons. She was patient. She sat at her piano and had me rehearse each finger placement and note on my flute to match her, which taught me how to train my ear.

I found pure joy in learning how to read a new language: music. Nothing was more satisfying than learning how to read notes on a page, blowing air through the flute, and producing sound. I am thankful for her for many reasons but mainly because she taught me about the diaphragm. The diaphragm is an umbrella-shaped organ resting under the lungs. It is the major muscle involved in respiration.

When playing the flute, you take a deep, deep breath until you feel like your belly button is about to explode. Then, you get the challenge of transmitting that air through a steady stream from your *embouchure*. It taught me to feel strength at the very core of my body. Through instructions of terms like *vibrato* and *tonality*, she taught me how to use my air to take up space. And, I tell you, she changed my life when she taught me what *dissonance* meant.

Living with my father's sister and her husband exacerbated feelings of worthlessness within me. Unlike my mother, my so-called caregivers rarely took the time to affirm me. I underwent neglect in the form of not having regular doctor or dentist visits or even birthday celebrations. For two hours each day, my so-called caregivers would lock me in the downstairs bathroom and force me to practice the flute.

I had such fear of the retribution I faced if I tried to open the bathroom door and escape to the room I stayed in without permission. I clearly witnessed the disappearance of my brother after he spoke up for himself. I did not want to disappear, too. I set my sheet music up on the bathroom sink and read the notes in preparation for my Saturday lessons. I rehearsed the thirty-six minor scales, trying to add them to my memory—trying to forget the life I once knew. Trying to forget the faces of my family members whom I thought I would never see again. Each day, I played until my fingers grew comfortably numb.

After a series of misfortunes, I began overhearing conversations regarding court, caregivers, and custody. Turns out, my mom was fighting to regain custody of me this whole time! I had no idea! I was so angry at my dad's sister and her husband. At no point did any adult ask me what I thought of my situation. *Can't they see that I'm a thoughtful person? Do my grades not reflect that I have a functioning brain? Don't they know I miss my brother, my best friend, more than anything? As a kid, am I just supposed to sit here meekly while my soul writhes at the loss of my entire family structure?*

A lady came by from what I thought she called *DeeFacts*. I later understood that she was using the acronym DFACS, which stands for Division of Family and Child Services. We walked around the neighborhood as she asked me questions like, "Do they treat you well?" and "Are you happy here?" I wondered to myself, *What really is "happy"?*

N Quail Drive

My mom organized her life to prove to DFACS that she was worthy of regaining custody of her children. I never got to visit my brother when he was away, and I learned that my mom was incarcerated for only four months. When I grew up, I found out more details of her case and that she was incarcerated because she was at a gas station when a white man verbally assaulted her by calling her a nigger bitch.

In defense of her dignity and sacredness as a southern Black woman, she fought him. But our three-year separation was because my mom was working to show the court that she was what is legally considered a fit parent. This included finding a job that would produce enough income to rent a house where each child has their own room with their own bed. This meant that as a formerly incarcerated woman, she had to work hard to find a three-bedroom home and, on top of that, acquire furniture. My dad's sister and her husband kept all of this secret from me.

I believe that my mom regained custody of me because I finally learned that I had *agency*. Whether or not my caregivers were telling me this, the law is done in the best interest of the child. One way to keep a child from expressing what they think is in their best interest is not sharing with them what is going on at all. Had I been given the opportunity to stay with my mother, who I knew loved me, I would have chosen that over the abuse and neglect I faced at the hands of my caregivers in a heartbeat.

When I chose to live with my mother, it's as if I noticed the sun shine brighter. I did have my own room, but I still had things stored at my former so-called caregivers' home. When it was time to retrieve items, we were instructed that they were in the garage. When the metal doors eased up, my mouth gaped open at the sight of my bedspread, my toys, and other prized possessions right next to two dogs, reeking of their stench. My mother held my hand before we gathered the items and went back to our new home.

I was not allowed to be part of the trial for my brother. If I were able to reverse time and find a way to take the stand, I would've

13

used my *diaphragm* to scream at the top of my lungs that he didn't deserve to be labeled as a bad kid and that not only is he brilliant, but he is also awesome. Instead, I was put in a separate room, where I waited.

That was the happiest day of my life at the age of nine years old. My mom came to where I was, in tears, and explained that she got us back. She explained to us that she had a good job where she was making seventeen dollars and fifty cents per hour and that we did not have to suffer anymore. I thought we had it made!

A different lady, who my mom very clearly told me was our case manager, came by again to verify that the house was up to par to legal standards. We lived in a three-bedroom, two-bathroom home, where everyone had their own bed, per the guidelines of DFACS. My mom exceeded their expectations. Mom affectionately referred to it as "the brick house." She was so hype about it that it made me think, *Wow! Bricks are awesome! Houses are awesome!* With my dictionary's help, I learned about architecture, which introduced me to the concept of *bricolage*. It basically means putting together whatever materials you can find to make a solid structure. I began to think that that is what life was all about.

My mother always had the news on, and I began to hear the reporter Monica Pearson talk about a *recession*. Having no idea what that meant, I carried on finding joy in making new friends at yet another new school, finding ways to continue to make good grades, and enjoying time with my mom and brother.

One day, I returned home to see my mom in what I felt was a puddle of her own tears. She explained to me that she was laid off from her job due to the company cutting costs as a result of the recession and that we would have to move again. *Bye, bye, brick house.*

Lovvorn Rd

At this point, I was in the fifth grade and moving to a small town called Mount Zion, which is located near Carrollton, Georgia. My mom explained to us that our house was located in a mobile home community. She explained that we would be safe in the Tall Pines community.

In this community, I met a lot of different kids who sounded completely different than my old friends in Douglasville. Most of the people spoke in long, lovely drawls, and I found myself training my ear to understand them. I still had no real concept of poverty because if I was able to have a shower and a meal, then I was satisfied. I didn't know that living in a "trailer park" was something that people think is to be ashamed of. I was grateful to have a semblance of structure. I was grateful to finally have my mom and my brother under the same roof.

My first birthday celebration after I reunited with my mom is a memory that I reminisce about with awe. My mom treated the day like my own personal holiday. She allowed me to invite all of my new friends to Cici's Pizza. Pizza was a long-loved cuisine in our household, so I was over the moon. She treated us all to the buffet of my favorite food and led everyone in singing "Happy Birthday to You." I felt loved and celebrated. The cheerful singing of the Happy Birthday song makes me blush to this day.

On the weekends, my brother, who was a senior in high school, would walk along the highway about half a mile away from the mobile home community with me. We would go to the gas station, buy snacks, and journey back home, and I would read, watch anime, and watch him play video games.

One balmy afternoon, on my daily walk down to our home, I enjoyed the sound of the gravel echoing beneath my feet and the warmth of the sun on my skin. About two homes away from mine, five neighborhood boys were outside playing, and they stopped to look at me. I waved at them. Much to my chagrin, they were not in a friendly mood in the slightest. They slowly began throwing objects at me.

First, a few hard gravel rocks, and then a water bottle. Because I had to pass by them to get home, I genuinely pleaded with them to stop throwing objects at me. They were persistent threw a firm basketball at my head. In the moments that I recovered from this, all five of them surrounded me and began hitting me. My rage and my fight instincts immediately kicked in, and I grabbed the smallest boy and defended myself. Very quickly, the pelting from the boys stopped. I ran across the street to a neighbor's house in tears and confided in them. They welcomed me in and called my mom.

Because this was in the afternoon and my brother had track practice, my mother was originally on the way to pick him up. When she arrived back in the neighborhood after receiving the call, she had a massive stick as thick as a baseball bat in tow. Once I identified who the boys were, she had me behind her and the stick in hand as she went to their home. After three knocks on the door, their mother answered. I remember my mother telling the woman that just because her boys witness abuse in the home, it does not mean that it is okay to treat girls the same way. She warned that if this were to happen again, the consequences would be devastating.

The woman retorted, "Is that a threat?"

My mother, with her effortlessly cool demeanor, icily replied, "No. It's a promise."

She turned swiftly on her heel, and we marched down the steps back into our home. She didn't even need to resort to physical violence with the stick! Her words were enough, and I never saw those boys again. From then on, I knew my mom would *always* protect me and that true respect is not acquired by harm or force.

I felt really fulfilled in school—except for in math class, since I vowed to always hate it when I was in the third grade. Even though I had an A, I never made an effort to understand it. My English teacher was a woman with a short, blonde pixie cut who really believed in me. She would give students Dum-Dum lollipops if we were on our best behavior. The sweet, tangy tangerine flavor quickly became my favorite.

After the annual Criterion-Referenced Competency Tests, she told me that I'd made the highest writing score in the region. I had no idea what that meant and was more concerned about if this warranted an infinite amount of tangerine lollipops. But seeing her smile at my accomplishment made me happy. I began to feel like I would be really successful if I kept learning about how to write exceptionally. Soon, my brother graduated from high school. I remember beaming with joy alongside him, and as he held his diploma with pride, I held his red graduation cap with a cheeky grin.

At the end of the school year, we moved from the trailer park and into a house that was directly beside it on the same street. One day, I woke up and found that my mom was not home, which brought back some feelings of *trepidation* familiar to me from years prior. My brother explained to me that he had to take her to the hospital because she'd had a heart attack. *Hospital?! What is a HEART ATTACK?! Why did no one tell me?!* I felt angry thinking about how my dad's sister did not let me visit her in the hospital last time.

When my brother and I got to the hospital, a Black man with kind eyes shielded by round glasses explained that he would serve as her cardiologist and told us that our mom had survived a stroke and two heart attacks due to a blood clot. My mom admitted that she was having chest pains and could not function at work, but pressed through her pain until it became unbearable. They diagnosed her with *congestive heart failure*. She was forty-two. I didn't have to open my dictionary to understand that that was a death sentence. My heart was shattered.

She expressed true gratitude that she was able to live through that trauma. The doctors sent her home with a long list of foods that may help her live longer, like lentils, leafy greens, and brown rice. All of that sounded yucky to me, but I began to marvel at my mom's resilience. I began to hold disdain for the definition of that word, as it is rooted in how much pain we can endure. This was the start of my awareness of the importance of health, restoration, and holistic healing.

My mom began to open up more to me about her life and what she endured. Here she was after four months of incarceration and over three years of arguing for custody for her children, proving to the legal system that she was indeed a fit parent, only to lose her work due to the collapse of an economic system—a survivor of traumatic health issues having the audacity to engage in conversations about faith.

Mt. Zion Road

Moving into yet another home, I began my sixth-grade year and the second school year under my mom's care. I finally got to learn more about her. I learned that she was an experienced model, actor, and flutist. I had no idea! She would tell me, "Demand the best from yourself, as others will demand the best of you." She spent a lot of time affirming me and letting me know that whether I won or failed, she would always love me. As such, I made it my mission to always excel.

I began heavily listening to rock 'n' roll music in middle school. My mother was an artist and drew inspiration from many mediums, whether it was the church choir, the drama theater, a stand-up comedy segment, the marching band, or a beautiful painting. She was familiar with most of my favorite artists, and she explained that in the '80s, the radio stations were not as segregated as they are today. So, she got to listen to many talented artists and bands, such as Joan Jett, Led Zeppelin, The Pretenders, The Doors, Van Halen, Metallica, AC/DC, and Duran Duran.

As a fellow musician myself, I was captivated by how music allowed these so-called rock stars to channel their energy into producing what I perceived as their own unique expression—some with gaudy eyeliner, leather jackets, sparkly blouses, tattered jeans, and hair teased out as if to defy gravity.

Upon further research, I found that rock 'n' roll music was originally created by Black people. This sent my love for the genre into the stratosphere. I learned about the true stars of rock 'n' roll: Billie Holiday, Sister Rosetta Tharpe, Willie Mae, B.B. King, Chuck Berry, John Lee Hooker, Little Richard, Tina Bell, Mother's Finest, and Jimi Hendrix. These artists were not using music to act "crazy" or be "wild"; they were reflecting on their positions in life as individuals who endured strife. Witty lines blanketed under phantasmagoric guitar riffs, mesmerizing bass lines, and rhythmic drum fills. All composed to tell a story of someone trying to make it through. All composed to attune sound to the soul.

I became hyper-focused on establishing my own identity through fashion. Lurking on the internet and engaging with social media introduced me to a punk subculture referred to as emo or *scene*. To align with the early 2000s scene trend, which was obscure in my rural town in 2010, I wore every color of skinny jeans that you could imagine. I donned brightly colored graphic tee shirts. I wore fake glasses with the lenses popped out, and for good measure, I put a Hello Kitty bandaid across the bridge frame. I rocked studded belts and cut off the fingers of my gloves. I think I genuinely wanted to be *seen*.

Looking back, my colorful self-expression was probably a result of wanting to mask the immense emotional pain that I'd endured the summer before. I began to notice small changes in my mom's well-being. Though she was physically able to function, we learned that her stroke had left her blind in her left field of vision. It became increasingly hard to sit alongside her at doctor's visits because I began to understand the gravity of her situation. I did not know how to process my fear and instead coped by going to the skating rink every week, writing, practicing my instrument, and having sleepovers with my new best friend in Mount Zion.

This was the beginning of my adolescence. Playing the flute in the middle school concert band paid off when I was invited to join the high school's marching band. The high school was a very small Title I school, and the band program was underfunded, as many are around the nation. The band genuinely needed more people, and a flute is essential to any ensemble. The band director was impressed by my eagerness and my talent. When I brought the permission slip to join the high school band, my mother signed it with a smile.

I remember writing an essay titled "If I Were Mayor of Mount Zion" for a contest presented during my English class. I dreamed up a world where I helped the town obtain consistently paved roads and grand architecture alongside a landscape adorned with flower gardens. I wanted the environment to deflect from the bleakness of the environments I survived— a true Utopia. To my surprise, I won first place and received my first cash reward for writing. It was a whopping two hundred dollars, and although I wanted to spend that on a shopping spree at rue21 to support my affinity for *scene* fashion, I am sure most of the money went to my mom to pay for bills, but that did not stop her from allowing me to get two new graphic tees and skinny jeans. I felt honored that my new community actually affirmed talent within me, and I am grateful that my mom supported my artistic self-expression without stifling me.

Pinnacle Way

At the start of my seventh-grade year, my mother moved us to Pinnacle Way. As a seventh-grader, I only hoped that we would experience stability. My mom referred to this house as her mini-mansion and was extremely happy to live there. The first day we moved to Pinnacle Way, my mom let me decorate my room with black splatter paint and plaster posters on the wall.

I had one of my favorite art pieces, *The Great Wave off Kanagawa* by Katsushika Hokusai, right above my bed. Other posters included Notorious B.I.G.'s *Ready to Die* album cover, a cutout of the Wu Tang Clan symbol that I remixed by coloring the background purple with "WUTANG" in block lettering, a *Breaking Bad* promotional flier given to me by a friend, and a still from Quentin Tarantino's *Pulp Fiction*. Out of all of the places we lived, this room became my sanctuary because my mom gave me the space to decorate it exactly how I wanted. I would retreat here to read, do homework, play video games, practice my flute freely, and scroll aimlessly online as an avenue for escapism.

At the end of each school year, my mom attended my awards ceremonies. She would beam with pride and cheer loudly, not only for me but also for my peers, making sure I celebrated each accomplishment with gratitude and joy. Before I knew it, it was time for me to prepare to graduate high school. Plagued with feelings of anxiety, I had no idea what institution to choose to further my education. Although I spent a lot of time enjoying my education, I never really envisioned anything beyond high school. In the fall of my senior year, I chose to apply to the University of Georgia and to Spelman College.

When informed of my acceptance into both institutions, and when Spelman invited me into the honors program, my mother beamed with pride. She became increasingly involved in my decision process and took me to tour both places. I was invited to the University of Georgia for their diversity day, and I was shocked to see that I was the only Black person in the room. The campus was large and sprawling, and I could not imagine taking a shuttle to get to each building.

I honestly did not know much about Spelman College, although Mount Zion rests forty-five minutes west of it. When invited for the admitted students' day known as Spel-bound, I learned more about the school and enjoyed being around fellow brilliant Black women. One day, my mom called me out of my sanctuary to watch an interview on TV. It was with former Spelman College President Dr. Beverly Daniel Tatum. Enthralled by her discussion on race in education and the assimilation of Black youth in white neighborhoods, I felt deeply understood and began to envision myself as a Spelmanite. We did not have the funds to pay for tuition out of pocket, so my mother and I joined hands in prayer. We decided that if it was meant for me to attend, I would be able to go. A helpful cousin was willing to pay for the admission fee, which I am grateful for because it was an exorbitant amount of money for my mother to pay while maintaining a home on her own.

My senior year of high school deeply saddened me. I feared the loss of the community that I had established over eight years. I found joy in my extracurricular activities that encouraged me to make interpersonal connections because as a child, I would only be able to know people for a few months before moving. Some of these activities included marching and concert band, writing for the yearbook staff, reviving and editing the school newspaper, and serving as a manager for the soccer team. I was part of a community that loved me enough to vote me as "Best All Around" for my senior superlative. When I probably should've been happy, I was stressed when I was informed that I was in the top one percent of my graduating class. I wanted to be valedictorian because it would have shown me that all of the turmoil I went through was worth it. Before I knew it, I was on stage in all white, delivering a salutatory address. Looking back, I am immensely grateful. For a child to have triumphed in the manner that I did, it is no small feat. Gazing into the crowd of my hometown, I choked back tears at my high school graduation and said farewell to people I knew I would never see in the same space again. The summer after, I worked long hours at rue21, making seven dollars and twenty-five cents an hour to afford decorations for my dorm room and to establish a sense of responsibility. Finally moving from Pinnacle Way was bittersweet; I had no idea what survival would be like on my own.

Amped Up

After a string of traumatic events that I survived during college before COVID-19 sent all students back to their homes, my post-traumatic stress became all-consuming. While in college, I self-soothed by smoking copious amounts of marijuana. I genuinely felt like I would never be understood by those around me. Even if the people I was around while in college studied the school-to-prison pipeline, knew the criminal justice system, or labeled themselves as social justice activists, most of them would never understand what it was like to live through those structures. Most of them would never understand how someone could remember such vivid details or what it's like to have those dark memories come back to you right before trying to get rest at night. I felt like I did not want to live if every day involved me fighting with the past. After getting very high for days on end from what was found to be synthetic marijuana, which I did not know at the time, I underwent psychosis.

It became very hard to fight the negative thoughts berating me, and I began to listen to them as they said that I did not matter. I began to believe that I deserved the molestation I went through; that I should be ashamed for keeping it secret; that I deserved the sexual abuse I survived in college because I did not report the man to Title IX; that I deserved the social isolation I felt because, ultimately, I did not matter. Not to my friends, not to my family, and especially not to God. Clearly, I was hard to love. I mean, how could I not be? Look at my life. I went through so much turmoil, rejection, and strife—and for what? So, I told my mom everything that I survived in the three years away from Pinnacle Way. I even finally told her about being abused as a child. She was devastated and hurt for me. Though she consoled me and encouraged me to continue therapy, I began falling deeper into suicidal ideation and depression engulfed me. My attempt involved me taking all of the medication prescribed to me and hoping that I would pass away in my sleep. My chest pain became unbearable, and I thought that it would happen for me. I called my brother to let him know. When my mom was informed, she immediately called the police, and I was subsequently hospitalized.

My mom came to visit me in the hospital rather than making me feel like I burdened her, which I eternally express gratitude for. I felt so regretful and guilty for causing her so much stress. I didn't want her to feel like she failed. I just didn't know how to live without letting my pain consume me. I was only ten years old watching her fight for her life on an eighty-inch hospital bed. Ten years later, she was watching me do the same. She held my hands and told me that I can't die because CVT, Inc. would not be the same. While I lay on my bed, she asked me if I knew why she loved butterflies. I told her that I couldn't remember. She told me the story of the caterpillar that completely dissolves itself while inside of the chrysalis. After time and within darkness, it undergoes a complete transformation before turning into a beautiful butterfly and flying on. I reflected on that and realized that I *would* be able to move beyond this moment. I realized that once you hit rock bottom, the only direction you can go is up. Once my heart was stabilized and the damage was not determined as too severe, I was transferred to another hospital for recovery. While in the hospital, I listened to a woman with cancer talk about how she overcame drug addiction. Her story was similar to mine in the sense that she used substances to escape traumatic memories. I asked her how she moved on from the past, even if she was hurt by people. She looked me straight in my eyes and told me, "You can't let them win."

When I was released from the hospital, instead of relying on psychiatric medication, I explored holistic healing modalities like breathwork and yoga. At the time, I was enrolled in an inaugural summer program hosted by one of the top universities in the country. I had taken about three weeks off due to my attempt. I was able to not only finish the program, but I was also given a superlative award titled "Most Outstanding Comeback." To this day, I am unsure if they knew why I had to take a long break, but that showed me that I am capable of recovering. I made it my mission to show my mom that my life would not be lived in vain.

Six months later, she called me on my twenty-second birthday to sing to me. She told me that I was the best daughter she could have ever imagined. She thanked me for always striving to do my best. She mentioned that my brother and I made her very proud because we did not succumb to the expectations people had of us. I thanked her and carried on with my day with the excitement that the following day was my brother's birthday. I wrote a lengthy post on social media for my brother to see, and my mom called me to let me know that she thought it was really kind. When she called me, I was with someone. Admittedly, I was terse because I wanted to continue hanging out. My mom quietly said, "You're being short. We can talk later." That was our last conversation. I am working on forgiving myself for not calling her back because she passed away three days later. I remember she said that without me, CVT, Inc. would not be the same. She never could have prepared me for the broken heart and void I felt without her.

When I think of my life, I realize that God blessed me with phenomenal favor in the best way possible. My mother was a woman with an indomitable spirit, which rang true even in her passing on. Even though it hurts not having her physically here or never being able to pick up the phone to hear her voice again, God used a legendary woman to serve as a vessel to bring me amd my brother into this realm. In my mom's lived experience, twenty-two was a traumatic year in her life due to her being assaulted and thus carrying my brother. She chose to protect him and continued to triumph through life while relying on the evidence of things not seen.

God orchestrated this so incredibly that her children's birth dates succeed each other with a perfect seven-year age gap. The number seven often reflects the fullness of completion. I watched, for years, as she worked fifty to sixty hours while having a chronic illness to maintain her shelter and basic necessities. After being given five years to live, she nearly doubled her life expectancy, living for just under ten years. My mother was much more than a conqueror. Her extraordinary perseverance is what makes her my lifelong inspiration. Her journey was deemed complete when her daughter turned twenty-two. In her own experience, that age also changed the course of her life. Even her memorial service was in alignment with divine timing, as it took place on February 13, the same date as her late sister's. Though harrowing, tell me, is that not phenomenal?

There is no darkness that light cannot overcome. Hold yourself accountable for the times that you were not living as the fullest version of yourself, and know that you are forgiven. Everything you lost will be restored to you if you keep the faith. Stroll with grace, knowing that you are redeemed. Allow yourself to cry. Even Jesus wept. He wept when he felt and observed the sufferings of God's beloved children. As God's beloved child, you deserve that cathartic release when acknowledging your trauma. The Bible repeats one phrase three hundred and sixty-five times: Do not be afraid. Confidently live each day unbound to the burdens of the past. Have the courage to love yourself enough to not participate in your own self-destruction. This is how I Raq 'n' Roll.

Every day is a flex on the old me. I live my life not in fear but with a spirit of power, love, and self-discipline. My healing heart trusts that God will use me for a purpose greater than myself. When my mom passed on, I was fraught with confusion, distraught on how to live without her physical presence. But now, at the age of twenty-four, I confidently lean into what she would advise me to do under any circumstance:

Rock on.

Raquel Thomas

Chapter 2

SECOND LEASE ON LIFE

This is dedicated to my parents, Jenel and Roy; my siblings; my family; my friends; and all the prayer warriors who kept me going against all odds. And to my daughter, Chelsea, and son, CJ . . . my two miracle babies.

June 30, 1989, is the day that began my "second lease on life." I am truly a walking miracle of God's phenomenal favor and a living testimony of the power of God, the power of prayer, and the power of positive thinking. My faith in God escalated and matured to the highest level back in 1989, when I experienced a tragic, life-threatening accident that changed my life forever. According to medical experts, I should have been dead and gone . . . but GOD had other plans. In the words of Pastor David

Jeremiah, "If you're not dead yet, you're not done yet." I am still here on purpose, with a purpose.

Just a Girl from Claxton

I was born and raised in the small Southeast Georgia town of Claxton. Claxton, Georgia is world-famously known as "The Fruitcake Capital of the World." The Claxton Bakery is a local family-owned bakery that began in 1910 and ships the "Claxton Fruit Cake" all over the world.

My mom, Jenel, and dad, Roy, were very supportive and encouraging and made sacrifices to ensure that I was able to thrive in school, achieve personal goals, and be the best that I could be in everything that I did. I grew up in a blended family with three sisters and six brothers (a total of nine children). My grandmother, Sarah, was very inspirational in my upbringing and helped to raise me from an infant. She was a woman of very strong and unwavering faith. She shaped many of the beliefs and values that I have in my life, especially my faith in God. My grandmother lived to be ninety-nine years old. She instilled in me what I call "Sarah's Pearls of Wisdom," which are: Have faith in God, be kind, and work hard.

With Claxton being a very small town, we had only one elementary school, one middle school, and one high school. So, the school-aged children grew up together like family. I developed a close circle of girlfriends, and we called ourselves "The Awesome Angels." We were high achievers, leaders in our class, young leaders in our community providing community service, active in our churches, and well-rounded socially. We were truly like sisters and made all sorts of plans for our future and adult lives.

One major goal we established while in high school was that when we turned the legal age of twenty-one, we would go to New York City (the Big Apple) to bring in the New Year watching the "ball drop." We held close to those plans throughout high school and even when we went off to college . . . but when we turned the legal age of twenty-one, God had other plans.

ATL Here I Come

After graduating from high school in 1986, I migrated to the big city of Atlanta to attend college at Clark Atlanta University (CAU), formerly Clark College. Crystal, one of my closest friends from the Awesome Angels crew, attended CAU along with me. We were so excited to be in the "big city," which was a huge change for us, coming from our small hometown of Claxton. Atlanta was very inspiring. Clark Atlanta University was very eye-opening; it helped to develop us culturally and prepared us for the "real world."

I had many aspirations for my college career. I was very active in extracurricular activities while pursuing my degree in business education at CAU. Cheerleading was my sport. I began cheering in fifth grade, cheered all throughout high school, and continued as a cheerleader while attending CAU. I received a partial cheerleading scholarship and served as co-captain of the squad my sophomore year and captain of the squad my junior year. I was initiated in Delta Sigma Theta Sorority, Inc., and was able to continue my passion for community service. I remained on the merit list for academic excellence, was initiated in honors societies, served as a Resident Assistant in the dorm, and landed an internship working with the Bureau of Wholesale Sales Representatives in Atlanta as an Assistant Office Administrator. Life was great; I was very proud of my accomplishments and was on track to graduate from Clark Atlanta University in May 1990, on the four-year time frame . . . but God had other plans.

The Peachtree 25th Building Fire

In April of 1989, I landed an internship with the Bureau of Wholesale Sales Representatives in Atlanta as an Assistant Office Administrator. I was twenty years old and in my junior year at Clark Atlanta University. I was very excited about this opportunity, as it provided me hands-on experience, utilizing the skills I was learning in my degree program. I started out working part-time hours; four hours per day, three days a week, and then began working full-time during the summer break starting mid-May 1989. I had great coworkers who were eager to help me learn, grow, and develop professionally.

It was Friday, June 30, 1989. I got up and got dressed for work, putting on my red blouse and cute black pencil skirt. I was happy it was Friday because I was traveling home to Claxton for the weekend after I got off from work. I arrived at the office at my scheduled 9:00 a.m. start time. I settled in and started my workday.

At 10:25 a.m. is when it all began! Our office suite was located on the sixth floor of the building. We had a power surge in the building, and the power had gone out. I went to the front of the office to speak with the receptionist. The electrical panel box was right outside of our office's front door. We had our office door wide open. A maintenance worker was standing in front of the electrical panel box, making repairs.

All of a sudden, a series of explosions occurred at the electrical panel box. The maintenance worker was immediately engulfed in flames! Toxic black smoke rushed into our office suite. I could hear the maintenance worker yelling and screaming for help, rolling, and kicking on the floor, trying to put out the fire that had consumed his entire body.

The thick, black, toxic smoke continued to hurl into our office suite. Some of my coworkers and I ran into one of the back offices and closed the door, trying to escape the excruciating heat from the electrical fire flames and the toxic smoke. We closed the door to the back office, as well, but the smoke was too powerful and made its way into the room. One of my coworkers managed to use an office chair to bust out the windowpane. We were seeking any kind of relief we could get.

The last thing that I can remember from being in that room was sitting on the floor, hanging my head and arms out of the broken glass window, gasping for air, yelling for help from the sixth floor of this burning building . . . the Peachtree 25th Building. A total of five deaths occurred because of this fire. One of the fatalities was a woman from my office. She had taken me under her wing and became my mentor at work.

The Fall from the Sixth Floor

My memory of the actual fall from the sixth floor of the burning building is totally erased. I do not remember a single thing between the time I was hanging out of the broken glass window, gasping for air, and when I woke up in the Intensive Care Unit in the hospital. I was told by my coworkers that I jumped out of the window, falling six stories (approximately sixty feet) onto solid concrete pavement. There had to be a team of guardian angels with me that day. It is truly a miracle from God that I am alive to share my story.

Video footage of the Peachtree 25th Building fire and me falling from the window was captured. The incident made national news, and I was called the "Bionic Woman" by the *National Inquirer*. Many stories from many people were shared with me about what happened during and after the fall from the sixth floor. A gentleman who came to my rescue when I landed on the concrete pavement saved my life by waving down the fire truck to stop when they pulled onto the scene. The fireman was not aware that my body was on the ground and was pulling in the fire truck full force to lift the ladder to save those that were still trapped in the building. If it had not been for the gentleman waving his arms and telling them to stop, the fire truck would have run right over me.

I was taken by ambulance to the emergency room of Piedmont Hospital. A team of medical experts was called in to assess my injuries and take action to try to save my life. According to my medical records, I responded by blinking my eyes. I had diminished reflexes in my arms and was observed to not move either leg. I had absent knee jerks and absent ankle jerks, no foot reflex was observed, and I could not wiggle my toes. My upper extremities revealed deep lacerations and blunt injury to my left hand. My pelvis was shifted, and I had a tear to my bladder, a tear to my uterus, and a lumbar spine fracture. My tibia was protruding through my right ankle with bone loss. I had a fractured fibula, and my left heel was crushed.

From this accident, I suffered many injuries, physical trauma, disability, and disfigurement. I have 15% permanent partial disability to my body as a whole as a result of my spine fracture, and 32% permanent partial disability of my right leg as a result of my ankle fusion. My doctors shared with me that when I arrived in the emergency room on the day of the fire, several of them, deep down inside, were thinking, *She is not going to survive this!* But God had other plans!

The News Hits Home

Meanwhile on Friday, June 30, 1989, back in my hometown of Claxton, my parents were at home, preparing for me to arrive for the weekend. My dad was outside doing some things around the house, and my mom was inside the house doing some cleaning. My mom had the television going on in the background while she was doing her cleaning.

She said she overheard a special newsbreak come on the TV that stated a building fire was happening in a downtown office building in Atlanta. It also stated that there were people trapped in the building waiting to be rescued. Then, the reporter stated, "One woman has jumped from the sixth floor of the burning building."

My mom said she began thinking to herself, *I hope that is not "Boote"* (my nickname that they call me) *in that fire. She works in an office building in downtown Atlanta.*

She said she went outside and told my dad what she had seen and heard on TV. Then, immediately after she finished telling my dad, they heard the house phone ringing. She said her heart dropped because she just knew it was a call from Atlanta.

Sure enough, when my mom answered the phone, it was a call from the Piedmont Hospital in Atlanta. The hospital had her identify her relationship to me, and then they shared the news of the tragic accident that had occurred and informed them that I was in ICU in Piedmont Hospital, and they needed to arrive as soon as possible.

My parents went into rescue mode and had to make it to Atlanta! A dear friend of the family gathered them both and high-tailed it to Atlanta from Claxton (a three-hour drive). When they arrived, they were in disbelief at what they saw. I had been put in a medically induced coma, with my body wrapped in medical bandages, drainage tubes inserted, and medical devices hooked up everywhere.

Dim Prognosis

The doctors reviewed my extensive list of injuries with my parents. The predicted outcome was very dim. My many injuries were going to require multiple surgeries and a long road to recovery if I survived the traumatic experience. The doctors said I may not walk again, and if I did, I would probably have a limp. I may not be able to have children due to the major internal injuries, and I would probably be hospitalized for several months . . . But God had other plans!

This news was devastating to my parents. However, they remained focused, kept a positive mindset, and sent up many prayers. They put their faith in God, trusted that He was in total control, and rested in knowing that His will would be done.

My Village of Support

The support I received from family, friends, college peers, sorority sisters, medical professionals, and even strangers was simply amazing. My support system was a key ingredient in my healing. I was blessed and highly favored with a village of outstanding support.

My mom took a leave from her job and moved to Atlanta to stay with me full-time while I was in the hospital. She advocated for me with the medical professionals and protected me from negativity. She would not allow anyone to come visit who did not have a positive spirit. She did not mind putting people out of my room or using a few "choice" words if she had to.

She bathed me, fed me, rubbed me, prayed for me, read positive affirmations to me, and took me outside for fresh air when I was able to get into a wheelchair. She lifted my spirits on the days I became sad and depressed. Pity, sorrow, self-doubt, and negativity had no room in my hospital room! My mom was not having it at all. I will be forever grateful for her unconditional love, personal sacrifice, and prayers which helped me to heal and sustained me through one of the most difficult times of my life.

My dad was the travel warrior. He had to continue working back home during the week to keep some income coming in while my mom took a leave from work. He traveled back and forth from Claxton to Atlanta every single weekend to visit while I was in the hospital. He would arrive on Friday evening and return home to Claxton on Sunday evening.

My dad does not like hospitals, and it was gut-wrenching for him to see me in the condition that I was in. When I would be in severe pain and crying, he would have to leave the room himself to cry. He never wanted me to see him crying, but I was very well aware of what was going on. I am so grateful for my loving, caring, and supportive dad. He has always been a great provider and protector for our family. His love for his children is beyond measure, and we are so blessed by God to have him as a father.

My siblings were my prayer warriors. One of my older brothers, Reginald, who is now deceased, was in the military and stationed in England. He and his family happened to be in the U.S. on vacation. He received the call that I was involved in an accident and quickly made his way to the hospital. He had to lay his eyes on his little sister. He was very much like my dad; he had great love for his family and was a protector. I love and miss my brother dearly to this day. He is now one of my guardian angels in Heaven, and I know he continues to watch over me and protect me.

My Awesome Angels crew was on point with prayers and support. My best friend and roommate, Crystal, was there through thick and thin. She was a huge relief and support for my mom, stepping in to help without hesitation. She, too, was an advocate for me with the medical professionals. She has always been an avid reader and tends to know a little something about everything. She did not mind asking questions and keeping the medical professionals in check. She also fed me, bathed me, and cared for me just as my mom did. She kept a positive spirit and quickly dispelled any untruths about my well-being that seemed to surface from time to time from those who did not have access to me.

My college peers, professors from CAU, sorority sisters, the Hagans family, and many others from my college life were tremendous support to my mom and me. They provided my mom with food, supplies, and things to help comfort and uplift her during her stay with me. They were prayer warriors for me and kept me lifted in spirit.

A was blessed with an A-1 medical team at Piedmont Hospital. They called in top experts from various medical fields to provide the best health care for me. They were very attentive to my needs and transparent about my health and progress. They did not give up on me.

The news about the Peachtree 25th Building fire spread all over the world. I received so many cards, well wishes, teddy bears, flowers, phone calls, and prayer vigils from strangers all over the world. Prayers avail much. I was blessed with positive spirits coming from everywhere. It was all part of God's plan. The world was able to witness His miracle work.

The Road to Recovery

I experienced many mixed emotions during my road to recovery. It was very hard, painful, depressing at times, and, most definitely, life-changing. I literally was Humpty Dumpty, who had a great fall—but unlike Humpty Dumpty, I was put back together again.

Many critical decisions had to be made about my healthcare, from major surgeries and blood transfusions to future care, etc. The expert medical team honored their roles as doctors, put their best foot forward, and did everything they could to put me back together again. We prayed and consulted God on every decision made. God was in control and provided His divine covering and protection through it all.

So, the tragic event occurred on June 30, 1989. I was twenty years old. I turned twenty-one on July 8. Well, that changed our Awesome Angels' plan to go to New York for New Year's Eve to watch the ball drop when we turned the legal age of twenty-one. Instead, I turned twenty-one in the hospital and spent the remainder of the year recovering and fighting to get back to some sense of normalcy in my life. Nevertheless, I spent New Year's Eve, at age twenty-one, watching the ball drop on television, at home, in Atlanta.

The doctors predicted that it would probably be about four to five months before I would be released from the hospital. I would be released to go home with surgical pins in my right ankle and left heel, and a pelvic brace on my body. I still would be unable to walk and would have a few more months of waiting before the surgical pins, brackets, and brace could be removed.

I had to lay flat on my back due to the pelvic brace that I had to wear to correct my shifted pelvis. The medical staff would come in daily to lift me and turn me over on my side to empty and clean the drainage tube that was in my lower back, relieve my back pressure, and avoid bedsores. I had to use a spirometer, a breath measurement device, routinely throughout the day and night (every two to three hours) to help keep my lungs open and avoid getting pneumonia.

I hated that device with a passion. It was a real struggle to breathe into the device and get the ball to rise to the desired level. I literally would cry sometimes when they came into the room for me to do the exercise. It was a daily challenge to stay positive with all the medical routines I had to do to help me heal. My mom continued to be that resounding voice to keep me in a positive mindset and strongly encouraged me to keep the faith.

I was placed on various opioid pain medications to deal with the excruciating pain. I began to become addicted to pain meds. I was given percocet, demerol, morphine, oxycodone, codeine, and hydrocodone—all of the highly addictive opioids. I was weaned off the opioids and provided more non-addictive pain medication, which included naproxen and gabapentin. In the midst of it all, God was still in control.

I went through eight surgeries for my injuries. I had a skin graft from my right thigh to cover my ankle because of the fusion surgery which reconnected my right foot, ankle, and leg. The surgeries lasted anywhere from four hours to thirteen hours.

My body responded appropriately to the surgeries, and I was miraculously able to be released from the hospital in August of 1989. This was approximately two months after being admitted to the hospital. I had already begun to beat the odds. The doctors predicted that I would be hospitalized anywhere from four to five months; instead, I was home in two months . . . Look at GOD!

I was transported home via ambulance service because I went home with the pelvic fixator brace, a surgical brace on my right ankle, and pins in my left heel. A hospital bed was delivered to my home prior to my arrival. That bed was like a Cadillac, a spaceship, and it had all of the bells and whistles on it for me to adjust the mattress to bring me as much comfort as possible. I was also provided a visiting home nurse who came in twice per week.

I was very thin in weight. I had dropped down to 102 pounds. Throughout my life, I was a healthy person with great muscle tone from the many years of cheerleading. This was depressing to me. I always thought I was "fine as wine," and you couldn't tell me otherwise. I was looking forward to the day that I could begin physical therapy to rebuild my strength and body. I was determined to be even finer than before. I began to speak it and claim it.

I had to return to routine follow-up doctor's appointments to assess the healing of my injuries, take X-rays, and ensure my surgery pins were clean and not infected. Going to my doctor's appointments was labor-intensive. I had to be transported via an ambulance each time because I still had the pelvic fixator brace and pins in my ankle and heel. I would be extremely exhausted after my doctor visits.

I continued to make progress with my healing. In September 1989, the pin was removed from my right ankle and replaced with a cast. The pins were removed from my left heel and replaced with a boot. I also finally got the pelvic fixator removed. I was now able to be transported to my doctor's appointments via a regular vehicle. I no longer needed ambulance transportation. I was on the mend as God continued to work His plan.

Physical Therapy

In October of 1989, I was scheduled to begin physical therapy. I attended three days a week for partial weight bearing to begin learning how to walk again without any assistance. I was looking forward to getting started.

Now, my very first day of physical therapy was the worst experience. It was the very first time that I had to stand straight up after being bedridden for four months. My first task was to get up out of my wheelchair and stand, holding on to the parallel bars. The physical therapist assisted me in getting up. I immediately became extremely nauseous, was sweating profusely, and almost passed out! It was a terrible feeling. I wanted to sit back down and not get back up again. I was informed that this was normal due to my months of not standing up, and it would get better as I continued physical therapy.

I prayed about my situation at physical therapy. I asked God to give me the strength, courage, and endurance to take on this physical therapy. I knew I had to do this. Besides, I had to get my "fineness" back and become FINER than before. So, that was also a motivator to get her done!!!

I continued a rigorous physical therapy program. I could see myself getting stronger and stronger every day. I attended therapy sessions three days a week and had routine exercises to do at home, as well. I completed six months of physical therapy.

Learning to Walk Again

I learned to walk again at the age of twenty-one. After months of intense physical therapy, I strengthened my legs and accomplished the goal of walking again without the assistance of anyone or anything. I went from being flat on my back with pins and braces all over my body, to a wheelchair, to a walker, to two crutches, to one crutch, to a walking cane, to finally walking again on my own. I am truly a walking, living testimony. God is SO AMAZING!

Beating the Odds

I defied and beat all odds that were against me during my near-death experience. Man said one thing, but God said another. The doctors predicted:

» I would be hospitalized for four to five months.

- » I may not be able to walk again.
- » If I walked again, I would have to wear a shoe lift or have a limp due to my ankle and foot injuries.
- » I may not be able to have babies or carry them to full term due to my internal injuries.

My full faith and trust in God sustained me and led me to His will for my "second lease on life." I BEAT THE ODDS:

- » I was released from the hospital in two months.
- » I was able to walk again.
- » I do not have to wear a shoe lift, nor do I have a limp.
- » I was blessed to have two beautiful, healthy children: a daughter, Chelsea, and a son, Chandler. I was able to carry them both full-term without ANY medical complications.

I was able to return to work in March of 1990, starting out working part-time with two full days per week. By June of 1990, I was back at work on a full-time schedule, exactly one year after the tragic event occurred in June of 1989. I also returned to school full-time in August of 1990 and completed my final year of college. I graduated from Clark Atlanta University in May 1991, with cum laude honors, receiving a bachelor's degree in business education.

ALL PRAISES to GOD! He had other plans for me to fulfill on this earth. He was not finished with me yet.

Life Lessons

I am a firm believer that everything happens for a reason. We may not always understand "the why," but God does. I can relate to this via two of my favorite scriptures:

Proverbs 3:5

"Trust in the Lord with all your heart, and lean not on your own understanding."

Jeremiah 29:11

"'For I know the plans I have for you,'" declares the Lord, "'plans to prosper and not harm you, plans to give you hope and a future.'"

I put my total trust in God during this very difficult time in my life. My faith and belief in Him became stronger than ever. No matter what prognosis the doctors made, I did not let it overtake me and become my source of truth. God is my ultimate resource, and He has the final say.

The three key lessons I learned from this experience that have stuck with me to this day and continue to be guiding lights in my life are:

1. The power of God
2. The power of prayer
3. The power of positive thinking

The Power of God

God is faithful and true to His word. He has the power to do supernatural and divine things. Nothing is too big for God. If we just trust and believe in Him, allowing His will to be done, He will deliver. I put my full trust and belief in God for healing and complete recovery during this tragic experience in my life. I am a walking miracle, a testimony, and evidence of the power of God.

The Power of Prayer

Prayer has the power to transform lives. As a believer, it is my connection to communicate with God.

Philippians 4:6–7

"Do not be anxious about anything, but in every situation, by prayer and petition, with thanksgiving, present your requests to God."

During my ordeal, I prayed to God day and night to heal me; give me strength; help me make the right decisions; surround me with positive energy; cover my doctors with skilled hands to successfully perform my surgeries; and cover and protect my parents, family, and friends, giving them strength and courage and helping them to keep the faith.

I was blessed to have intercessory prayers being lifted for me from people all over the world—those known and unknown. Prayers avail much, and I am a witness to what the power of prayer can do in your life.

The Power of Positive Thinking

"You are what you think."

"So as a man thinketh, so is he."

How we think will manifest our reality. If we are thinking negatively, our behaviors align with our negative thoughts and, ultimately, deliver a negative reality. Positive thinking can have a beneficial impact on both physical and mental well-being. Research has shown that people who maintain a more positive outlook on life cope better with stress, have better immunity, and have a lower risk of premature death.

I focused on having a positive mindset while going through this life-changing event. I am very grateful for my mom, who continuously reinforced positive thinking. When there were times that I may have been slipping, she was right there to bring me back to reality and focus on the positive. I know that my positive mindset in this tragedy helped me to have a victorious outcome. My behaviors aligned with my positive thoughts and resulted in a positive reality. In my daily life, I intentionally focus on thinking positive in all that I do.

Living with Purpose

By God's phenomenal favor and grace, I am still here! I am extremely grateful. I was chosen to still be here to live out my purpose of paying it forward and making a positive impact in the lives of others. I have continuously been able to do this via leadership in my sorority and empowering the communities we serve, implementing community service programs in my hometown of Claxton, and through giving back programs in my professional workplace. It is personally rewarding and fulfilling for me when I have been able to assist someone with a need and make a positive difference in their life.

I will continue to pray every day that God guides me and leads me to ensure that I am living according to His plan. He kept me here to do just that with this second lease on life.

Cassandra Hayward Hines

Chapter 3

DARE TO KEEP MOVING

*This chapter is dedicated to my family, friends,
and all those who have experienced hurt,*

then dared to hope, dared to forgive, and dared to live:

You are proof that light will always prevail.

There's this inspiring West African Proverb, "A man who does not leave his hut will bring nothing in." As you go out in this unpredictable world, go where God leads you. When in life you feel stuck, it is my prayer that you will lean into your courageous side and dare to move on. Here's my journey . . .

Move-In Day

When I was born on Christmas Day in 1966, my parents were seventeen years old! When my dad graduated from high school, he joined the United States Army. His first duty station was in Germany. When I was six months old, my mom and I moved to be with him. I don't remember much about being in the house with both of my parents because they divorced when I was two years old. Before the divorce, my brother, my only sibling, was conceived in Germany. Before he was born, my mom and I moved back home. I did not see my dad again until I was ten years old.

As a young child, I felt rejected by my dad and did not understand why he did not come back for his family. I quickly learned that I needed to help my mom with my brother, and it would always be the three of us. Our mom did an amazing job in raising us as a single parent.

One afternoon when my brother was four, he was asleep on the front porch—or so we thought. My mom tried waking him up, but he would not. She called 911 and the operator told her to open his mouth and give him a teaspoon of sugar because it sounded like he may have a drop in his sugar levels. My brother was rushed to the hospital, and on the way, he had a seizure. He was later diagnosed with "juvenile diabetes" and had to stay in the hospital for weeks. Our mother could not miss much work, so she returned after a week. Therefore, I had to stay at the hospital with my brother. I learned to watch over him and get a better understanding of his medical condition.

My brother learned how to give himself insulin shots; he learned that he could not eat sweets regularly, and his favorite soda at that time was "Tab"—which was filled with sugar. I know some of you have never heard of that soda, as it has since been discontinued. My brother always said when he was younger that he would join the Armed Forces after graduation. His dreams were shattered when he entered the ninth grade; he was told by a recruiter, "Because you are insulin-dependent, you cannot join the Armed Forces." He did not let that damper his spirits and decided to do other things.

At this time, I was in the eleventh grade playing three sports (basketball, softball, and volleyball). My brother was not interested in playing sports, and our mom was not interested in allowing him to play sports due to his medical condition. We had developed an unbreakable bond. We loved to be together, so he decided to become the boys' varsity basketball manager. This meant he and I were together every day after school during my practices and on game nights. I could keep my eyes on him all the time. He graduated from high school and started a career in fast food.

My brother became a hard worker, dedicated, and humble. I could not have asked for a better brother. We loved each other, and he thought his big sister and best friend could do no wrong. As he continued in the fast-food industry, he became a manager and worked from open to close several days a week. One day on his way to work, he stopped at the local CVS drug store to get some orange juice. When he returned to his car to leave, someone saw him slumped over the steering wheel. He'd had a heart attack. He was rushed to the hospital, had triple bypass surgery, coded three times, and recovered, by the grace of GOD. He was eating greasy fast food every day at work and not taking his insulin as prescribed. He was married when this happened, but his wife did not stay committed to her vows and walked out on him while he was fighting for his life. I believe, in my heart, that he did not fully recover from her leaving him. The couple had two children, and he had a daughter from a previous relationship.

Our mom became my brother's caregiver again, and they moved in together. He could no longer work or drive. He had suffered nerve damage throughout parts of his body, and his insulin amounts increased. This meant he was taking three to five insulin shots a day. Due to the amount of insulin that had been injected into his body over the years, his body became immune to insulin, and he had to take insulin to live from day to day. He eventually had to have five of his toes removed, which caused him to wear specialized shoes. He never complained about his life.

He never said, "Why me?" My brother embraced his situation and lived his life for his three children. I was hurt when I noticed my brother not being himself, not remembering things, not making complete sentences, and his hands shaking while feeding himself. Although my brother had suffered physically and emotionally, he showed us how to weather the storms of life. God truly favored him.

Unpacking My Faith

In 1989, I graduated from Florida State University with a bachelor's degree in criminology. After college, I started a career in law enforcement. I met someone in 1990, and we were married in 1997. In August 1999, I returned to college to obtain my master's degree and found out that I was pregnant. In May 2000, we welcomed the most beautiful, adorable little girl into our lives.

Having come from a single-family home and not having my dad around, I wanted different for our daughter.

In 2002, we moved to be closer to my husband's parents, who were getting older, as their health was deteriorating. Having lived in a big city, I was excited about the move. In addition, we wanted our daughter to be able to go outside and not wonder if she would be a victim of gun violence due to the high crime rate in the city that we were relocating from. However, before I left, I had a conversation with my brother about my leaving. I explained to him that moving would not change our relationship, and whenever he needed me, all he had to do was call. I also finished my master's degree in public administration from Troy University that year.

When we moved, our daughter was a year and a half old and growing up right before our eyes. She had a strong personality and was determined to figure things out on her own. I would read to her daily, so much so that when she got older, she loved to read and conduct research on any topic. She was taught that knowledge is power, so as a reward, she would get a new book at least every two to three days. Our bonding time would be to go and get a new book; she would read it and later tell me what it was about.

When she got in trouble for not cleaning her room, talking too much in class, or not doing minor things when told to, I would say, "You can't watch TV." Her response would be, "Okay, I will read my book." She became an avid reader at school and home to the point that we had to get a membership at Books-a-Million.

As parents, we did not force any particular activities on our daughter; she had the opportunity to find out what she liked to do and what made her happy. With that being said, she knew that whatever she wanted to do, once she started it, she had to finish it until she said, "No more." Her first interest was dance, and she was six years old when we were introduced to a dance studio in our new hometown. She has never been shy, and she could talk with the best of them. She attended dance class with other girls her age, but she was the tallest student, so she would have to stand in the back. That did not last long.

As she began to enjoy dancing more and more, I told her that to have a spot in the front row, she would have to work twice as hard as anyone in the class. That meant giving 110 percent at rehearsal and working on her craft when no one was watching. As time went on, she eventually moved to the front row and made the competition teams. We would travel to different cities and states for dance workshops and competitions. This was our mommy-daughter bonding time.

While our daughter was enjoying her time dancing, I decided to return to college again to obtain my Ph.D. in criminal justice. What was I thinking? *Here I am, a wife and much older mother of a six-year-old, working full-time, and now, I am a part-time student.* I went back because I have always wanted to own and operate a domestic violence shelter for women.

During this time, my husband was working as a car salesman, and on some weeks, he worked fifty to sixty hours with one day off. That meant him being at work more than being at home. Our daughter noticed that her dad was not attending her competitions; he only made it to the end-of-year recitals. At a young age, I could see the disappointment on her face, but I would let her know that he was out providing for us, and that was why he missed her events. Although her dad missed out on a lot of her events, they had a very close relationship. He taught her how to hunt and fish, and that was their time of bonding.

However, as she got older, dance became her life, along with cheering, other after-school activities, and dancing at church. She always wanted her dad to see her accomplishments and be proud of her. She wanted him to take her to her practices and pick her up, go on daddy-daughter dates, talk to her about how a man should treat her, and be her number one guy in the world. He never drove her to any of her practices, even when he was off.

The two never attended a daddy-daughter dance, and he never talked to her about how she should be treated by a man. She got to a place where she no longer expected her dad to do those things that she felt a dad should do for his daughter. She could always count on me; I would rearrange my schedule to accommodate her schedule. I have never missed a dance competition, dance recital, dance workshop, cheerleading tryout, football game, or basketball game. There were many times when I felt that I was a single mother living with a husband and the father of my child.

Whenever her dad would show up, they would make eye contact, and her face would glow with a smile. However, her expectations of him became different as she began to notice his lack of participation when it came to her. To put that in perspective, she would say, "I know my mom is not going to miss any of my events. Not sure about my dad." She felt the same type of rejection from her dad as I did with my dad.

God, Do You Have the Right Address? Where Are You?

When she was fifteen years old (2015), our lives—my life—changed. In October, I had an appointment with my OB-GYN, who has now gone on to be with the Lord. He was the best when it came to bedside manners. Before I would get undressed for an exam, he would come in and have a seat. He would ask how everyone was doing. We would talk a little about our families and life in general. We would discuss the purpose of my visit and what would take place during the exam, and he'd ask if I had any questions.

This time, I explained to him that I had noticed some blood in my stool. He said, "Get undressed, and I will be back." He conducted the exam, and when it ended, he said, "Get dressed, and I will be back." Upon his return, he said, "I am going to write a referral for you to get a colonoscopy. People usually have one at the age of fifty, but you are close enough." I was forty-eight at the time. He did not go into detail as to why I needed to have a colonoscopy, and he did not discuss what to expect or not to expect from the exam. We talked a little more, and he gave me the referral.

I went to my scheduled appointment and met with the gastroenterologist who was going to perform the colonoscopy. I explained the situation. He said, "Get undressed. When I return, I will have to numb your rectal area to proceed with the colonoscopy." Mind you, I had only heard of a colonoscopy but never knew anyone who had one done. The doctor returned, gave me a shot, and told me he was looking for colorectal polyps.

I said to him, "What is that, and should I be worried?"

He replied, "Colorectal polyps are small clumps of cells that form on the lining of the colon or rectal area and cause bleeding in the stool. They could develop into cancer."

Fear began to take over my mind and body. The procedure was over. I was instructed to wait out in the lobby; someone would come and get me once the results were back. As I waited, I began to pray over my body and say, "I have divine health, and no weapon formed against me shall prosper."

The test results showed that I had polyps, and I was then diagnosed with colorectal cancer, also known as colon cancer. What is colorectal cancer? I'm glad you ask—it is defined by medical professionals as a growth of cells that forms in the lower end of the digestive tract, and it is hard to detect, yet it is a very dangerous form of cancer.

After getting such devastating news, my flesh immediately went into fear mode, and I could only think about my daughter. I began praying and saying, "Lord, not now. I cannot leave my baby. She needs me." I was the first person in my family to have any form of cancer; therefore, I did not know what to expect.

I got myself together and continued to speak with the doctor to find out where to go from there. He stated that I had a tumor in my rectal area, but he was not able to tell the size, and that I needed to schedule an appointment with a proctologist, a colorectal surgeon, to have the tumor removed. My OB-GYN passed away before I could give him the results.

I was given a referral, then I left the office and went to my car. I started crying, praying to God that He would not take me away from my daughter. I knew I had faith and that I believed in God, but I still was wondering why He chose me for such a thing as this. I called my husband and told him that I had cancer.

I did not get the response I thought he should have given me. I don't know if it was fear or what, but I was expecting more compassion. I told him I was going home, and he did not say he would join me. At that moment, I felt alone and confused. While the drive home would normally take me twenty minutes, it seemed like my house was much farther away that day, which allowed me more time to talk with God.

While I waited to get an appointment with the proctologist, I started to develop pain on the left side of my body from the waist down. I contacted my primary caregiver, who stated that I could be suffering from sciatic nerve pain. He gave me a referral to seek physical therapy, which lasted about four weeks. It did not relieve the pain; it was just wasted time and money.

By November, the pain became unbearable to the point where it was difficult to sit down or sleep. I can remember the many nights I slept in the guest room so that I would not keep my husband up or wake up our daughter. I would scream into the pillow because I was in so much pain. I barely slept five hours a night, I would sit on a pillow to drive, and while I was at work, I would sometimes stand at my desk. It was like the least amount of pressure on my rectal area would feel like pins and needles just shooting through my body, and there was nothing I could do about it. Although I was in constant pain, I refused to allow our daughter to see me in pain.

My husband and I were finally able to meet with the proctologist. As we walked into the office, my spirit became unsettled, and things did not sit right with me. The first thing I noticed as I began to take my seat was the doctor's lab coat. It was not pure white and clean. It was dirty.

I began scanning the office and observing other things that made me uncomfortable. Mind you, I was in pain, so I could not sit long as we discussed the purpose of my visit. When he sat down at his desk, he immediately slammed his doctor's reference book onto the table and said, "I don't know what you have been told, but with this type of cancer, you will have to wear a colostomy bag for the rest of your life."

A colostomy bag, also known as a stoma bag, is a pouch that is worn on the outside of your body to catch waste. This takes place when a surgeon makes a new opening in the abdominal wall, and a piece of the large intestine sticks out. This condition can be temporary or permanent.

I started to cry because I was scared and didn't know what he was talking about. I can remember getting undressed from the waist down and bending over a table with my rectal area in the air. To locate the tumor (cancer) and determine the possible size, he would have to examine my rectal area. He touched the outside of my rectal area, and I screamed, "No! That hurts!" The pain was so awful; I could not stand the touch.

After screaming, I got dressed, and we walked out of the office. Last but not least, his bedside manners were unspeakable. He showed no compassion, sympathy, or pure concern for what we were going through. I will always carry those feelings with me, and I believe to this day that God was telling me that he was not the doctor who needed to operate on me. Having a relationship with God allowed me the opportunity to hear His voice as I was dealing with this major decision in my life. I know that God speaks to us all in different unique ways, but we must know His voice, and when we don't, we take drastic steps that could cost us later.

I returned to work and explained to my coworkers what I had just experienced. They simultaneously said, "Go get a second opinion from the Mayo Clinic in Jacksonville, Florida." I called and scheduled an appointment with another proctologist at the Mayo Clinic. Again, this was all new to me, but I knew I wanted someone who cared about their patients and would explain what was happening to my body.

In the meantime, the pain began to get worse. I always felt constipated and was not able to use the restroom regularly. On November 20, 2015, I was able to meet with a surgeon at the Mayo Clinic. He explained in detail what was going on with my body and how he was going to help. He discussed that he had to conduct an exam and that it would be painful. The exam was performed, and it was very painful.

Afterward, he sat beside me and said, "Yes, you do have a tumor in your rectal area. I was not able to locate the entire tumor; therefore, I cannot determine the size." He went on to say that the only way to get the tumor out was to have surgery and that he may have to cut my splenic flexure out. The splenic flexure is located in the upper left abdominal area and helps with the flow of blood through the body.

He said, "I do have some good news: The cancer is only in stage II, and you don't have to have chemotherapy." I had heard so many horrible stories about chemotherapy and was very grateful that I did not have to experience it. I jumped from my chair and began doing a praise dance.

He explained that the tumor was the cause of the unbearable pain, but he would give me a prescription for it.

He went on to say, "If you want me to do the surgery, and if I have to cut your splenic flexure out to remove the tumor, you may have to wear a colostomy bag."

I said, "Yes, you will do the surgery."

I was no longer scared. I liked everything I had just heard, and I knew that I needed to rely on my faith. If God brought me to it, He would bring me through it (1 Corinthians 10:11). Again, I immediately thought about our daughter and how she would handle knowing her mother was suffering from cancer. Although she knew I was in pain, I made the decision not to tell her until it was the right time. I could not be selfish and allow what I was going through to affect her. All she had ever known was that her mother was strong, and she made things happen.

I took the medication several times a day, every day, but it did not help the pain. I was told that I was given the strongest dose of oxycodone, and there was nothing else that could be done until the tumor was removed. The day finally arrived—January 6, 2016, surgery day—and I had to be at the hospital at 11:00 a.m. for preoperative evaluation and preparation. I woke up celebrating this day. I knew that soon, the pain would be over, and I would have my life back. I made sure I had everything I needed, spoke with my daughter, and explained that I was having a procedure. I told her not to worry about me; I would see her after school.

The hospital was about an hour away from our home, and we were thirty minutes late. My husband was driving, and I felt that my appointment was not as important to him as it was to me. Again, he could have been fearful of the situation, but I never knew how he felt. Upon my arrival, I was immediately taken back to meet with the nurse. I was instructed to change into a gown with the back open. As the nurse got ready to start my IV (intravenous cannula), she said, "You have small veins, and I am having trouble locating one." She tried my right arm, but could not find one, so she called in another nurse.

While I waited, God spoke to me and reminded me of a song that I had heard on the previous Sunday at church by Travis Green, "You Made a Way." In addition, my pastor always had a saying: "It is already done." He would say those words no matter what people would tell him about situations in their lives. It was his way of encouraging us and letting us know that God was on our side. It was his way of saying to just trust God, get out of your feelings, walk by faith and not by sight, and know that this is only a test of your faith.

That nurse could not find a vein and went to get another nurse. Before she left, I asked if I could use her pen. I wrote those words of encouragement on my palms, and when the nurses returned, I told them that I was ready to get this over with. God gave me a chance to put my faith into action. He did not allow the nurses to find a large enough vein the first time they tried. The IV was placed in my right arm, and that was the last thing I remember before falling into la-la land.

Nine hours later, at around 10:30 p.m., I woke up from the surgery and yelled out, "My back hurts! Why is my back hurting? I did not have surgery on my back."

Vaguely, I heard, "She is up."

I was informed that the surgery had taken place on a metal bed that had a hole underneath my rectal area, and that was the reason my back was hurting. Remember the issue with the IV? Well, when I woke up, it was in my left arm and not the right. I asked what had happened because my right arm was bruised and swollen. I was informed that the vein had burst, so the IV had to be taken out and placed in the left arm. It took weeks for my arm to recover.

I stayed awake for a few minutes to be able to see my husband and my daughter, as I was dozing in and out of sleep due to the pain medication. She was crying and asking if I was all right. She asked why I didn't tell her that I had cancer. I could see how scared she was for me. I told her that I did not want her to worry about me because she had school, dance, and cheer to worry about. Although I was in a great deal of pain, I knew just by looking at her face that God had saved me to be the best mom I could be and that she needed me. She wanted to stay in the room with me but was not allowed. I explained to her that I was better and that I would see her before she left for school the next morning. She and her dad stayed in a hotel near the hospital.

My husband told me that he had spoken with the doctor and that the surgery had gone well. He said that my body was not the same. As the night went on, I was in so much pain, and I noticed that a tube was coming from my rectal area. I spoke with the night nurse, who provided me with medication and told me that the tube was a wound vacuum, a device that would remove pressure from the area of the wound and pull fluid from my body.

This House Does Not Feel Like Home

The next morning, my husband and daughter came to visit me. We spoke for a few minutes, and then they left to go to school and work. I've always wondered why he did not let her miss school and why he did not miss work on that day. I needed them both at that moment. I'd just had a whole surgery that resulted in a piece of my large intestine sticking outside of my body. I needed hugs; I needed them to hold my hands and assure me that everything would be fine. I wanted to feel like we were all going through this together, not just me. I know that if my daughter had the choice, she would have never left me. I was left in the hospital alone with no family—just doctors and nurses who were caring for me. That was one of the lowest points in my life.

As my surgeon made his rounds, he stopped by to see me. As he entered my room and got closer to the bed, I could see tears in his eyes.

I asked, "Why are you crying? What happened?"

He said, "I am so sorry, but I was not able to save your splenic flexure, and you have a colostomy bag." He also said that my rectal area, up to my private area, was completely closed with about forty-five stitches and that I would never be able to use the bathroom as a normal person. Just the way you are looking as you read this, that's how I was looking—in shock! That's what my husband meant when he said that my body was not the same.

My response to him was, "You don't have to be sorry. Did you get the tumor out, and am I cancer-free?"

He said, "Yes, and yes."

I said, "You have given me more time to be with my family, and I am grateful." We hugged and cried tears of joy.

He said that my tumor was the size of a small orange, and it had been growing in my body for the last seven years. I felt chills as I thought of what could have been. That meant that I had developed cancer when my daughter was eight years old. I continued crying and thanking God for not taking me away from her. Remember the unbearable pain? That pain came from the tumor sitting on a nerve in my rectal area. So, the more pressure applied to that area by my sitting, the worse the pain got. We discussed my recovery and what to expect as I started this new journey as a cancer survivor.

Toward the middle of the day, I met the most amazing nurse. She introduced herself and explained how to use the colostomy bag, told me where to order my supplies, told me about other resources, and encouraged me to keep my head up. In addition, she said, "Your life will not change because you have a colostomy bag. I have been wearing one for twenty-five years, and my life has not changed." Hearing those words from her gave me so much hope going forward. I knew that the road would be long, but I didn't feel alone at that moment. God had given me favor with Him, and *man*, which was phenomenal.

I was discharged from the hospital after three days with a recovery period of six weeks. This recovery included me having a home healthcare nurse who had to come every other day to change my bandages, and I had to continue wearing the wound vacuum until all the fluids were removed. This was not a good time for me; I was really in a dark and scary place. I fell into a deep depression, but I did not let anyone see it, and I did not share my feelings with anyone. I thought about my life before cancer and how much I enjoyed it. Again, even at this point, I was questioning God, asking, "Why me, God?"

He said, "Why not you?"

You are probably wondering how I went from being grateful to being depressed in a matter of days. Don't misunderstand me—I am forever grateful for God sparing my life and putting the right people in my life at the right time, but I still felt alone and confused. As you know, life is not always the same every day, so when I had to go home and face reality, I did not know how to handle it.

Our daughter continued her schedule with school, dancing, and cheering, and my husband returned to work two days after I came home. I'm not sure why he did not take leave and stay home with me for at least a week. At times, the pain and soreness were so unbearable, and I hated sleeping with that wound vacuum.

As I was recovering and healing, I remembered my home healthcare nurse talking to my husband one day.

"Let me show you how to change the bandages," she said.

His response to her was, "I'm good. You can do it."

He walked out of the room, and you can imagine how embarrassed I felt with the lack of support I received from him. I never looked at him the same, and our lives changed from that point on. I began to think about our vows, "For better or for worse; in sickness and in health." They were mere words at that moment. He made me feel as if it was my fault that I had developed cancer and that my body had changed. After about three weeks, I no longer had to wear the wound vacuum, and I could drive myself around. The home healthcare nurse stopped coming to my house once I was able to drive because my insurance would no longer pay for her services. I was told that I had to get my bandages changed at the local wound care center.

At the wound care center, I met another amazing nurse manager. We talked about my situation, and she explained that her sister was going through the same thing. Then, we started talking about where we lived and our children. Who would have known that we lived about five miles apart and our daughters were friends?

The nurse said, "Let me help you so that you don't have to pay a copayment to the wound care center on your next visit."

I immediately did a praise dance and said, "Look at God."

She said that she would come to my house every two days and change my bandages—now, *that's* phenomenal favor. We developed such a close bond, and I owe my speedy recovery to her. I saw my surgeon after six weeks and he released me to return to work. It took me a minute to get used to wearing the colostomy bag, getting used to eating certain foods that would not affect my digestive system, and being a cancer survivor.

As a part of my recovery, I met with an oncologist, also known as a cancer specialist. I was told that I would have to have post-chemotherapy to stop any future cancer polyps. My reply to him was, "Why would I want to kill the good cells in my body? Do you have an alternative?" The alternative was that I had to have a computerized tomography (CT) scan every three months over the next three years and a colonoscopy every year. The purpose of the scans was to check if any new cancer cells had developed. I am proud to announce that I have completed the scans; I only have to have a colonoscopy every five years. As of January 2023, I am seven years cancer-free. I see you praising God for me!

He Moved Out, and Favor Moved In

Although I had survived cancer, my marriage went in a different direction. After about twenty-one years of being married, we no longer felt attached, and we were not happy. However, I was willing to attend marriage counseling, but he was not. So, on January 30, 2019, my husband got up and decided he no longer wanted to be married to me. I was sitting in the living room when he walked past me with his bags packed and said, "I am leaving." He did not tell me where he was going, but he did tell me he was not coming back because there was nothing for him in our home.

My heart dropped to my stomach, and again, I started thinking about our daughter. I thought about the sacrifices I had made for my family. Despite it all, I could now be getting a divorce. I could not imagine not being married and our daughter not having her dad in the home with her. I was devastated and started blaming myself for my marriage ending. I started questioning myself and my abilities as a wife. He has never said it, but I have always felt that he felt some kind of way about me having this stoma bag.

I asked God, "Why me? Why did I have to have cancer, and why did my marriage end?"

God responded, "Why not you?"

I was so angry, bitter, and disappointed because I wanted my marriage to work. I told myself that I would give my husband a year to come back home to discuss our marriage, apologize for his actions, and try and work things out.

At this time, our daughter was in her second semester of college, and she was devastated when I broke the news to her. She needed financial help, and her dad was not answering any of our calls. She began to ask herself, "Why doesn't my dad like me, and why did he leave me?" When I looked into my child's face, I knew I had to pick myself up. So, I joined the gym and had two amazing personal trainers. I worked out four days a week, at 5:30 a.m. and 5:30 p.m., for months. I took my frustrations out on the weights and the boxing bag. That was my release.

Our daughter started working two jobs while attending school, and I was working a full-time job and had picked up two part-time jobs so that she and I could survive. I worked those three jobs seven days a week for nine months until I could get back on my feet. I remember not eating for days, making sure that our daughter could eat and she had gas to attend class. I prayed to God for the strength and the ability to move forward and whatever His will would be for my life. I have always had a relationship with God, but when I went through my separation, I began to have a deeper relationship with Him. I began to understand Deuteronomy 31:8, "God will never leave me nor forsake me." There were times when I did think that God was not with me. I just could not understand how God could let His child go through this pain.

By December 31 at 11:59 p.m., I had not heard from my husband concerning our marriage. In January 2020, the world was dealing with the COVID-19 pandemic. Everyone had to shelter in their homes, businesses were closed or had limited hours of operation, and I was still dealing with my marriage. I decided to file for divorce and move on with my life because he had moved on with his. In March 2020, I learned that he had moved to another city and was sent divorce papers. Upon receiving the papers, he sent me a text that said, "You did not have to get lawyers involved." He did not attend the first scheduled court hearing. After being separated for about a year and a half and waiting on another court date due to the pandemic, I started to receive information that he had not been faithful to me throughout our marriage. I received phone calls and things in the mail concerning his infidelity. I wanted to confront him about the information I had received, but my attorney said she would handle it in court.

As I waited for a court date, I watched our daughter go into a deep depression, and I could not take the pain away. As a parent, you never want to see your child in pain. By this time, she was not doing well in her classes. She wanted to quit and come home to take care of me. She would say things like, "Mommy, if I quit school, I can work and help you with the bills." I told her that she could not quit school and that I would continue to do whatever it took to get us through these difficult times. One thing she has always done is trust me, and there was no way I could let her down. I had to fight for my survival along with hers. In no way did she deserve this. She was used to having both of her parents in the home together, she was used to getting the things she needed and wanted, and she was not used to suffering financially.

In November 2020, I received a call from a dear friend who said, "You need to sell that house, move away, and start over." I was thinking, *I'm in no position to move*, but my friend offered me a job with her company. I sold the house with no equity because he stopped paying the mortgage. The house needed repairs, which cost me money at closing. I packed my things and left town. I was ready to go to court and get this divorce over. The healing process was going well. I started to change the things I was saying about myself. I would say, "I did nothing wrong; he left me; he cheated on me; I am enough; I was a good wife and mother; I am worth it—always was, and always will be." The list went on and on until I knew that God had given me phenomenal favor within myself. I had developed a sense of peace. I was no longer angry or bitter; I was just done. The Lord could not bless me until I had forgiven him. I told myself that I may never get an apology, and I may never understand why he left. Trust and believe I will never forget what he did to me, our daughter, and our family.

On April 13, 2021, we met at court with our attorneys, sat opposite each other, did not make eye contact, and did not speak; all conversations were through our attorneys. My attorney told the judge that the two parties had agreed on the terms and that the proceedings did not have to continue. That was the order of the court. Just like that, our marriage was over. There are no winners in divorce.

I called our daughter and told her that it was over. She said, "Mommy, I am glad because he did not deserve you. You were a great wife, and you are a great mother."

Driving home as a single woman after having felt so much pain through this process, I felt a sense of release and relief, but alone. I felt like I deserved so much better in my life. I began to think about how my life would be going forward. I thought about how difficult it would be to meet someone and talk about having cancer and wearing a colostomy bag. *Will I ever find love again? Will I find someone who loves me for me? Can I trust someone again? Do I want to be in a relationship again? Do I want to be married again?* I had so many questions about how my life would look after divorce. Life after divorce is uncertain and scary.

I knew that no matter what was taking place in my life, our daughter still needed me. She was now in her last year of college, and she and her dad were not on speaking terms. I witnessed the anger she carried because she did not enjoy college life like other students; she was working to survive. She later revealed that she wanted to harm herself and had gone days without eating because she did not have food.

I asked, "Why didn't you tell me about these things before now?"

She said, "I did not want you to worry about me, and I wanted to make you proud."

As a mother, you can imagine how I felt when I heard those things from my child. I assured her I would always be proud of her and I loved her. I explained to her that no matter what, none of this was her fault, and I apologized to her for my part in it.

Although college life was challenging, she did not let those things stop her. God began to show her phenomenal favor by allowing her to change her major so close to the end of her college career without losing credits and only having to take a few extra classes. During those times, she admitted that she questioned God. We talked about how strong she was and how the enemy wanted to see her give up. I quoted to her John 10:10, "The enemy comes to steal, kill, and destroy, but God had come to give [her] life," and my favorite, Jeremiah 29:11, "For God knows the thoughts He thinks toward [her], thoughts of peace and not of evil, to give [her] a future and a hope."

By January 2022, things began to brighten up for her and me; we both were in a better place. Her dad started to reach out to her from time to time. She would say, "I love my daddy, and I miss him." As she began to forgive him, she asked him why he left us. He said, "I felt that your mother loved you more than she loved me." She asked why he wouldn't help us, and he said, "Because I was mad."

Our daughter graduated on May 6, 2022, from Georgia Southern University with a degree in psychology. She is doing very well for herself.

On December 29, 2022, the Lord gave me one of the most precious gifts I could imagine—a new grandson. When he arrived, nothing that I had experienced even mattered. He brought so much joy to our family.

Change of Address

When I thought I could not take another devastating blow to my life, on January 26, 2023, at 10:00 p.m., I received a call from my mom saying that she had to call the ambulance for my brother, and they were at the hospital because he had been coughing and throwing up. Having been used to my brother being in and out of the hospital throughout his life, I felt this time was no different. Usually, he goes to the hospital, they give him medication and keep him for observation, and my mother calls and says, "He is all right; he is back to himself." My mom told me to go to bed and that she would call me in the morning. I received a call from her around 3:30 a.m., telling me my brother had been admitted to the hospital. Again, I didn't think anything of it and told my mom to keep me posted. The following day at around 10:00 a.m., I received a call from my niece.

She said, "Grandma said to call you."

I asked her, "How is your dad?"

She responded, "Auntie, I don't know. He has all these tubes running from his body, and he is not responding."

I called my mom, and when she answered, she was crying. I knew at that moment something was wrong and I needed to go home. I did not want to upset her anymore, so I didn't ask any questions. I just told her that I was coming home, and she said, "No. You have to stay at work." I told her to give me a few hours, and we would be there.

The drive seemed longer than normal and I was worried about my mom and brother. I would not allow myself to think the worst. No matter what was going on, I knew I had to be strong for everyone. Upon our arrival at the hospital at around 6:30 p.m., Mom said that my brother was unconscious and there was an issue with his lungs. As I walked into his room, I met with several nurses and doctors. I looked at my brother with all these tubes running from his body, all these monitors beeping with numbers, and I knew things were not looking good. I had not seen him like this since he had his heart surgery. The doctor started saying words to us that we could not understand.

I said, "Can you break that down to me?"

He said, "Things are not looking good for him."

As family members came and went, my brother's immediate family stayed at the hospital until around 11:30 p.m., talking and praying with him. We decided to go home, shower, rest, and return at 8:00 a.m. for visiting hours. When we got home, we were so tired that we all fell asleep in a chair or on the couch. At 1:30 a.m., my mom received a phone call stating we needed to return to the hospital. We showered and went back to the hospital. Before our return, my brother had four heart attacks. The doctors told us that with each heart attack, he had coded, and they asked if we wanted him to be resuscitated if it happened again. They told us that he had lost oxygen to the brain, and if he survived, it would not be good. I signed the forms to not have him resuscitated. God showed us phenomenal favor by allowing us the opportunity to return to the hospital and say goodbye.

Within fifteen minutes of the forms being signed, we watched the numbers on the monitors go down, and my brother died. He waited for us to return before leaving us. The passing of my brother had stirred up a different kind of pain, and because I had been through so much over the last seven years, I handled it better than I thought. I started to remember the good times and how God showed him phenomenal favor time after time.

Dare to Move On . . .

"The great courageous act that we must all do is to have the courage to step out of our history and past so that we can live our dreams." — Oprah Winfrey

As my story ends, and as painful as things were in my life, I would not trade my life because I learned how to go through the storm of adversity and be able to tell others about the goodness of God. I have received phenomenal favor from God throughout other areas of my life. In that, He allowed me to experience marriage and divorce, raise a daughter into a beautiful young lady, survive cancer, watch my daughter graduate from college, witness my grandson being born, and survive the death of my only sibling. For that, I say, "Thank you, Lord."

As far as my Ph.D. is concerned, I have completed all the coursework and need to finish writing my dissertation on how domestic violence affects children in the home.

Without a test, there could be no testimony. Therefore, I will continue to walk by faith and not by sight and to trust God for continued phenomenal favor over my life, my daughter's life, my grandson's life, and my mother's life. As gospel artist Hezekiah Walker would say, "When I think about all that I have been through, I can't help but give God glory because He favored me."

"She was never prepared for half of what she went through, but she got through it."

She is me.

Alfaye Miller

Chapter 4

GOD WORKING
BEHIND THE SCENES

*Dedicated to my daughter, Imani; and every girl or woman who has ever
made mistakes, doubted, hesitated, or been rejected, hurt, or afraid.
This is written to give you hope.*

Setting the Stage / God as Playwright

Tears ran down my face and began to soak the neckline of my blouse as I looked out of the window at the sky and familiar landmarks while seated in the back seat of the police car. When we arrived at our destination, I attempted to get out of the car on my own, but I couldn't. I had never ridden in the back seat of a police car before. I didn't know that there were no door handles inside. The police officer came around to open the door. As he helped me to get out of the car and led me to the doors of the building, I wondered, *How did this happen? How did I get here?*

In a book about phenomenal favor, you may not expect to read an account of me being transported in the back of a police car. You may expect that my story will chronicle how I have been walking on sunshine and experiencing my best life all my life. While I have certainly been blessed in my life, the blessed life is not my entire story. I have had a series of disappointing and dysfunctional experiences. Those experiences eventually led to God's blessing and phenomenal favor. God loved me too much, however, to bless me with His favor at any time other than the right time and in any way other than the best way.

As I think about the seasons of my life, I imagine a brilliantly written theatrical production, with timing and action that only God could pull off. Critical parts of any live performance happen behind the scenes. As one scene proceeds, workers we don't see are offstage preparing for the next scene. This offstage activity happens before a production, during its run, and even after the production. I have come to realize that this is how God works. Throughout all my experiences, God was working behind the scenes. I didn't know, and I sometimes even worried about what was next. Journey with me to learn how God miraculously worked in a number of ways behind the scenes to bless me with His phenomenal favor.

Difficulty Fitting In / God as Sound Engineer

I come from humble beginnings, growing up the second of six children with our Mama and Daddy in a small town in Northwest Florida. We had what we needed and sometimes could afford things we wanted. I was raised as a Christian and continue to be an unapologetic follower of Jesus Christ. Daddy was a deacon in the church. Mama sang in the church choir and participated in many other church ministries. We were taken to Sunday school and church services almost every Sunday.

My oldest sister, Freda, was ten and a half months older than I. We were raised like twins, dressing in matching outfits and participating in shared life experiences for many years. We started kindergarten and graduated high school at the same time. Freda was outgoing, athletic, and popular. I was not.

I constantly compared myself to Freda and to others. It didn't help that relatives and friends also frequently made these comparisons. In my mind, when I compared myself to others, I always fell short. I was known as "the smart one" and "the quiet one." I made good grades, got assignments done ahead of time, and stayed out of trouble. Even so, I felt inadequate and wanted to be more like my sister and my friends. My feelings of inadequacy grew, and although they ran deep, I didn't have language for what I was experiencing at the time. Not only did I not have language for it, but I also felt that I had no one to talk to about it. My parents were certainly too busy raising my siblings and dealing with adult issues. My siblings and friends wouldn't understand and would probably think less of me if they knew what I was feeling. I didn't trust teachers or other adults in my life enough to share my innermost thoughts.

Another factor that I believed to be working against me at the time was that I was a "late bloomer" physically. By the end of middle school into early high school, Freda and many of our female friends had developed more physically than I, flaunting breasts and a figure. I was seen as "sweet" and "cute" by boys, like a little sister, not the girlfriend type.

Although, in recent years, I have come to recognize the value of therapy and have taken advantage of it. I could have benefited from therapy then to help me work through my feelings and develop strategies to cope. Therapy was not something people in my circle talked about or took advantage of at that time—not in my age group, not in my family, not at my school, not in my church, not in my community. It didn't happen. What happened was this:

By the time I was thirteen, I had developed such low self-esteem that I decided my life was not worth living. I had easy access to prescription medication that was prescribed to someone else. I had heard of people dying from accidental overdoses of medication, so I thought pills were a way out for me, although it would not be by accident. I began to steal pills over several months and hid them a few at a time so that they would not be missed.

I don't recall any particular incident that occurred the day I decided to take them. It was a Saturday afternoon. Once I thought I had collected enough pills, I took them, lay in bed, and fell asleep, expecting to die. I don't know how long I slept, but I woke up feeling violently ill. Stumbling, I made it to the bathroom and began to vomit. I vomited until it seemed there was nothing more in me, and then I vomited some more. My parents took me to the emergency room. After a brief examination, only checking my vital signs, the doctor casually chalked it up to a stomach virus. He didn't order any lab tests but prescribed something to calm my stomach and sent me home. Whatever damage the pills might have done—even ending my life—was not done because God, through His divine protection and favor, purged them from me. I did not talk to anyone about what really happened. My parents never knew that I did not have a stomach virus that day.

Even though I struggled with my self-worth and self-image, I had a relationship with God, and I talked to Him frequently during my childhood and teen years. I took to heart the Bible lessons I was studying, learning, and even teaching in Sunday school. I believe that sustained me after my pill-taking experience.

God was working as the Sound Engineer in this production, managing sound effects and experiences, so that instead of continuing to hear the negativity from others or even in my own thoughts, I began to hear the promises of His word. I continued to be the smart one, the quiet one, the cute one, and the sweet one. That is who I was authentically. It was enough, but I didn't know it at the time. As much as I could, I worked to not compare myself to others. I continued to do well academically and even had a couple of boyfriends later in high school.

After high school, I moved away to attend Florida State University in Tallahassee. College years were pretty easy. After all,

I was "the smart one." Although college was an enjoyable, exciting experience, I faced ups and downs and struggles from time to time. When dropping me off at college, before leaving, Daddy had given me a little metal box. Inside were about twenty scripture cards. I found during those years that the most valuable scripture for me from that box was Jeremiah 29:11: "For I know the plans I have for you," declares the Lord, 'plans to prosper you and not to harm you, plans to give you hope and a future.' I cherished that little box of scripture cards. Although the box eventually broke and had to be replaced, I still have the cards today.

Dangerous Liaison / God as Lighting Director

Several months after graduating college, I moved to Jacksonville, Florida to stay with a former college roommate. She lived there, working as a nurse, and had invited me to stay with her and look for a job. I had moved back home after college but had difficulty finding a job there. Daddy had recently passed away. I welcomed the opportunity to move to Jacksonville.

Not long after moving there, I found a job. When I began making enough money, I moved out of my college friend's apartment and rented my own place. I also met a friend of my friend; I'll call him Petty Officer because that was his rank in the Navy. He was a few years older and took an immediate interest in me. I felt special and savored the attention.

We began hanging out. We became friends. The relationship progressed quickly, and I became his "girl." Things progressed even further, and we got an apartment together. He paid rent and utilities. He bought furniture. He bought clothes for me. I only needed to buy groceries and household items.

Although the relationship seemed nice in the beginning, eventually, Petty Officer began to control who I saw, what I wore, where I went, and what I did when I got there. He took me around his friends as if I were a trophy. When in public or with his friends, he coached and coaxed me to show a little more cleavage, bend over at the right time, cross my legs the right way, touch someone "accidentally."

According to Petty Officer, I had the looks and the body but just needed to be "more sexy." I mentioned during my Difficulty Fitting In season that I was a late bloomer physically. Well, when I finally bloomed, I had an hourglass figure, with full breasts and hips and a tiny waist. That is part of the reason Petty Officer was attracted to me. He constantly complimented me on my looks and figure but also frequently reminded me of my shortcomings and what I needed to do better.

When Petty Officer was deployed with his squadron, sometimes out of the country, he would call frequently to ask me to describe in detail how I had been spending my time. He wanted particularly to know whether any men were paying attention to me and how I reacted when they did. It was bizarre. Because I was a young twenty-something and wanted to be accepted by him, I pretended to be someone I wasn't, doing what I could to maintain his approval. I didn't feel comfortable or safe doing what I believe he expected, so I made up stories to tell him.

After a couple of years of pretending, I asked Petty Officer whether we would ever get married. I had grown up in a household with married parents, and in my mind, marriage was the next step when two people were committed to each other. Petty Officer replied that, of course, we would get married when we were ready. He eventually gave me an engagement ring as a birthday gift and said, "You're really mine now." He wouldn't discuss wedding dates or plans, even when I tried to.

While I didn't clearly see it at the time, I came to realize that Petty Officer did not plan to marry me. Giving that ring was his way of keeping me where he wanted me. Because I was the easygoing, quiet type, he saw someone he could easily manipulate. The relationship was about control and dominance. He was grooming me to meet his warped needs. For nearly five years, he continued in his quest to mold me into someone I was not, and I tried to become that person. I looked forward to the times he was deployed away from Jacksonville, so I could be myself and feel comfortable in my own skin.

One morning as I was walking my cocker spaniel, Brandy, a gift from Petty Officer, a couple of women who lived in our apartment complex stopped me. They told me about how Petty Officer had continuously come on to and propositioned one of them when I was not around. As he did so, he would berate me and tell them that we were just friends, nothing more. All the while, his words to me were that he loved me, and we were going to get married when the time was right.

The women invited me to their church. I had not been attending church regularly and agreed to go, and I went with them the next Sunday. It was a good service. The pastor preached a message about God's love. I was reminded of that love that had followed me through my childhood, adolescence, and college years.

I realized that I had been looking for love in the wrong place and from the wrong person. I began to pray to ask God to help me escape that toxic relationship. I had developed a false sense of financial dependence on Petty Officer, which he had worked hard to cultivate. I could support myself with an adjustment to my habits and style of living.

Although Petty Officer controlled many aspects of my life, he didn't control my work and career. I had been promoted to district supervisor, and everything was going well at work. A few weeks after I began to ask for God's help to find a way out of the toxic relationship, a state leadership team from my agency visited my workplace. They spent a week checking in to see whether our district met state requirements. As they were leaving, one of the women on the team told me about an open position on the state leadership team.

She encouraged me to apply. Getting the job would mean I would have to move back to Tallahassee. I applied and was offered the job and a substantial pay raise. I accepted and moved to Tallahassee. Petty Officer was deployed in Iceland at the time.

The agency paid my expenses to move from Jacksonville to Tallahassee. It was not just a reimbursement of expenses, but they paid a moving company directly to pack my things, load them on the truck, drive them to Tallahassee, and unpack them. Other than gas for my car, I did not pay one penny for the move.

I still remember the feeling of freedom as I drove on Interstate 10 with Brandy, a few house plants, and, surprisingly, a frog in my car. I don't like frogs at all and didn't want the frog to make the trip with us, so, screaming, I pulled over, stopped, and coaxed (probably frightened) the frog to jump out of the window. I let out a deep sigh and giggled to myself. Brandy seemed to be giggling, too. It felt like I had been suffocated but could breathe again. I felt free, like that frog.

God's favor provided a way of escape for me. Just as a Lighting Director controls and produces light to create an atmosphere in a theatrical production, God's light helped me to see what I had not seen before. I had a new perspective. I could see who I was. I could see what love was and was not. I could see a path to my future.

It took a little while to completely break free of Petty Officer. After he returned from Iceland, there was a trivial matter of furniture items he had purchased that he wanted back. He also made one last attempt to win me back. In the end, he got the furniture, but he didn't get me.

Divorce / God as Stage Manager

My escape from Petty Officer brought me to a place where my career would thrive, and I would meet my first husband. Although I am unmarried as I write this chapter, I refer to him as "First

98

Husband" because God may be preparing me and the man who will be my next and last husband.

I met First Husband about a year after my escape to Tallahassee. We worked in the same office complex. We met one afternoon in the parking lot as I was getting into my car after work. First Husband often told the story of how, after that first meeting, he and a friend searched for me for days, walking every floor of the six buildings in the office complex until he saw me in a conference room in a meeting.

He did not approach me at the time because I was busy. He knew the car I drove, so he left a note on my car giving his phone number and asking me to call him. I called. We talked and arranged our first date. We hit it off. He made me laugh. He was so different from Petty Officer, my safe place to land.

Two years later, we were married. Two years into our marriage, our daughter was born. We shared in raising her. We adored her, and she adored her parents. She thought her mom knew everything, and her dad could do anything.

Our worlds were intertwined. We built a home together. We worshiped as a family in church. We even came to serve together in leadership positions in the church. In our professional lives, we usually worked in partner agencies or nearby buildings. We frequently called each other during the day to check in, say hello, or meet for lunch.

After many years of what seemed like marital bliss, things began to change. We no longer called each other to check in during our busy workdays. Lunch dates and date nights ended. We stopped participating in activities the other enjoyed. While we continued to attend the same church, we drove separately. We didn't sit together, and we barely spoke while there. Intimacy gradually decreased. He began to take frequent out-of-town weekend trips for poorly explained reasons.

One evening when I was feeling particularly frustrated, I let First Husband know that I felt alone and lonely at home, even when he was in the house. He spent most of his time at home in a separate room watching TV or in long phone conversations with someone. I told him that I might as well be living by myself.

He told me he took that statement from me as a sign that we didn't need to be together any longer. I tried to explain that I wasn't saying I wanted to be alone but was just communicating that I felt alone. He didn't hear me. I believe now that he was ready to go and was using anything he could to support his plan.

Over the next few weeks, he shared many complaints about me that he had never shared with me in more than twenty-four years of marriage. Most seemed to me to be petty, insignificant things. The one crushing thing he said to me was, "I never really loved you, anyway." NEVER. He said that he didn't feel what he thought he should feel for me.

He said he thought his love for me would grow after we got married, but it didn't. He told me that he was tired of pretending. Wow! With each word, I felt like I was a nail, and he was a hammer pounding me into a wall.

I was devastated as our nearly twenty-five--year marriage was ending. First Husband had a casual attitude about it, making statements such as, "We just grew apart" and "It happens." I suggested professional couples therapy, talking to our pastor, and other remedies. He declined all of it. He was done. Maybe he said those cruel things to me because he wanted to be sure I was done as well. It worked. I was done.

One of the many self-help books I read during that time advised that I write down the lies that were being told to me or that I believed about myself and, beside them, write the truth from God's word. I wrote First Husband's words on an index card, and beside them, I wrote messages from God's word: "I have loved you with an everlasting love; therefore, I have continued my faithfulness to you" (Jeremiah 31:3). "I will never leave you or forsake you" (Hebrews 13:5) "Before I formed you in the womb, I knew you. Before you were born, I set you apart for my holy purpose" (Jeremiah 1:5). I carried that card and frequently pulled it out to read it.

Although he initially denied it, I found out that First Husband had a relationship with another woman for at least the last two years of our marriage. She was waiting in the wings as my life was falling apart. If it had been possible for me to crumble into a thousand pieces and fall to the floor when I found out what had been going on, I would have. I didn't crumble, though. I held it together the best I could. The crumbling would come later.

It took only four months from filing for divorce to the final divorce decree. We reached an amicable settlement agreement without disputes or quarrels. Throughout the process, God was working behind the scenes as the Stage Manager, foreseeing what was next and preparing the way. He saw situations I didn't see and heard conversations I didn't hear.

He knew a bigger plan that I did not know. Experiencing a divorce after more than twenty-four years of marriage certainly took me by surprise, but it did not take God by surprise. While the divorce process was emotionally and psychologically taxing for me, God had gone before me to be sure that it wasn't a lengthy, prolonged process and that the tasks and actions were coordinated, organized, and completed in a timely manner.

Debt and Financial Uncertainty / God as Executive Producer

Debt had been an integral part of my adult life. Soon after graduating college, I received preapproved offers for credit cards from department stores, jewelry stores, and gas companies, including Montgomery Ward, Sears, JCPenney, Amoco, Exxon, Texaco, and Zales Jewelers. I accepted all of them and began to use them. It didn't take long for me to bring the balances for several of those cards to the maximum.

At the same time I was paying on those accounts, I also had a student loan that needed to be repaid. It was a relatively small student loan compared to the amounts people speak of today, but it was more than I could afford to repay given my other debts. I began making small payments on the student loan.

The amount I paid was less than the required minimum, but the lender accepted it. I paid what I could when I could on the other debts while enduring threatening calls from debt collectors unless I decided not to answer the phone or pretended to be someone else when I answered. I continued living in debt as I joined in marriage with someone who also had debt. Over the years, we managed credit cards, personal loans, home improvement loans, and debt consolidation loans.

As I was approaching the end of one phase of my professional life, preparing to retire, I knew I would soon be bringing home less money compared to my take-home pay as a state administrator. My retirement timeline was preplanned, but I also planned to be married when I retired. As I was facing divorce, I realized that not only would I be bringing home less in retirement, but I would also be living on one person's income instead of the two-person income I had grown accustomed to for twenty-four years.

In our divorce agreement, First Husband and I divided our remaining debt in a way we believed to be fair. I was worried about how I would make it financially and prayed continuously about it. I continued to give financially in church but was not always a faithful or cheerful giver.

More than thirty years of demanding work had brought me to a place of complete burnout, so the idea of getting another job after retirement did not appeal to me. I met with a financial planner and began to work on a short-term plan to pay down debt as well as a long-term plan for my financial future. My budget was tight, and I had wavering confidence in the plan. God had come through for me so many times before, and I wanted to believe that He would bring me through this seemingly impossible challenge. I prayed that my confidence in God would increase.

We decided as a part of our divorce settlement that we would sell our home. Although First Husband had input when the home was built, I had selected every brick, door, door handle, light fixture, tile, countertop, cabinet, faucet, floor, and paint color for that home. It was my dream home, and I mourned losing it.

As we were preparing to sell, I put a deposit on an apartment I planned to move into after the house sold. I prayed and sought God's guidance and was led to call our mortgage lender to investigate purchasing a home on my own. After asking a few questions and requesting a couple of documents, the company sent me a preapproval letter to use during my search for a home. I hired a realtor but started to look around on my own.

One sunny January afternoon, I was parked, sitting in my car and waiting for an open house for a newly constructed home to begin. A lady came out of her house across the street. I'll call her Lisa. She asked if I was looking for a home to purchase. I told her that I was. Lisa let me know that although her home was less than two years old, medical issues and life circumstances made it necessary that she sell the home and move. She was about to put the home on the market.

She invited me inside to look and pointed out several upgrades both inside and outside that were not included in the newly constructed home across the street. As I walked through, I could imagine myself living in the home. It felt tranquil and serene.

Lisa and I had the same taste in décor. We exchanged contact information, and I thanked her. My realtor showed me several homes. Although many were newly constructed, in my mind they did not compare to the two-year-old home Lisa showed me. It had captured my heart.

A couple of weeks after I met Lisa, her realtor contacted my realtor to let him know the home was on the market. I made the first offer. We agreed on a contract, and on a cold February afternoon, six weeks after Lisa first showed me the home, I closed on the purchase. Earlier that same day, First Husband and I closed on the sale of the other home.

I moved into my new dream home. My furniture fit just right. I met good neighbors. I felt comfortable and safe. Monthly mortgage payments for my new dream home were less than the amount I would have paid to rent an apartment. My tight budget loosened. It had been a very hasty, stressful six weeks, but God's hand and his favor were working throughout.

After living in and enjoying my home for about a year, I called the mortgage company one day because I was experiencing trouble updating my log-in password on the company website. The customer service representative helped me update my password, and after checking my file, he told me it appeared I was eligible for a refinance. Within a few weeks, I had refinanced my home, my interest rate was lower, and my monthly mortgage payment was hundreds of dollars less. Now that my budget had loosened even more, I was able to repurpose more freed-up funds to pay down my debt.

God's favor didn't stop there. As I was a few months into retirement and accustomed to what I believed to be my new income amount, I received a letter that the amount of one of my retirement income sources had previously been miscalculated. The payment should have been more than I was receiving, so I would begin to receive the new increased monthly amount and would receive a back payment to cover the previous months. I was able to pay off more debt. God is good! He remained faithful to me, even though I wasn't always faithful to Him.

Each time I was losing hope on the journey of debt and financial uncertainty, God showed up repeatedly on my behalf as the Executive Producer. An Executive Producer for a theatrical production is responsible for finding the money to finance the production and for managing the financial risks. God, my Executive Producer, has proven that He will supply all my needs and give me more than enough.

Depression and Anxiety /
God as Casting Director

By nature, I am a person who does well when I have a lot to do. In college, I excelled when I had a large course load. I made the dean's list only in semesters when I had large course loads. In my professional life, I excelled when I had only a couple of hours to write a comprehensive report or a few days to gather a team to complete a project. I pulled it off when I needed to sew thirty garments over a weekend for a church production or plan and organize an event. I got it done. If there was someone to help, that was fine. If not, I did it all by myself.

I lived life like the Energizer Bunny. I kept going and going and going until I wound down. Winding down typically manifested in the form of migraine headaches or digestive issues. After a brief hiatus to rest and get myself together, I would wind myself up and get moving again to meet the demands that awaited.

One of the most difficult experiences of my demanding life was dealing with the death of my sister, Freda. Freda, the one with whom I was raised as a twin, shared a bedroom, played make believe, styled hair, traded makeup, graduated high school, and talked about the joys and challenges of raising our children; the one who served as matron of honor at my wedding and I maid of honor at hers, passed away following the most valiant, brave, faith-filled fight with cancer that I have witnessed.

Several months after Freda's passing, Mama was diagnosed with cancer. After a two-year battle, she passed away. Mama was my greatest cheerleader, as she was with all six of her children. She made me believe I could accomplish anything. She never passed on an opportunity to brag about us to family and friends as she updated them on where we were and what we were doing. This was a great loss for me. I missed my Mama.

As I was trying to deal with those losses, my professional life became increasingly stressful. Although I was preparing for my planned retirement, I found myself overworked, overwhelmed, and overcommitted at work. As administrator of a statewide program, I was leading a large team in the office as well as people in locations across the state of Florida. I was carrying a lot of responsibility. At the same time, I held too many leadership positions at church.

Because I was leading while broken, things began to deteriorate. Friends I thought had my back were seemingly stabbing me in the back. I tried to carry on and meet all my responsibilities but felt unsteady, like all the connective tissue was draining from my bones and I would collapse at any minute.

While the divorce proceedings had gone smoothly, I was living in my new dream home, and my financial plan was working, things were not really settled for me. I had not found my new rhythm. I didn't know how to do this dance as a single person again and live alone after so many years living as a wife. I believed that my identity was tied to that role.

My mom and sister were no longer here, so I couldn't talk things over with them. My daughter was living on her own and didn't need me as much. I was trying to be a good example for her on how to handle being newly divorced, and I felt like I was failing miserably.

I had unprocessed grief and felt unsupported and alone. After searching for and finding a good Christian therapist, I completed a few sessions, was beginning to think I might find a light at the end of the dark tunnel, then took a break from therapy because I was too busy to fit it into my schedule.

I was juggling a lot, trying to keep too many balls in the air, disregarding my feelings and emotions, and everything came crashing down on what might have been a typical Friday morning at the office. I was sitting in a difficult meeting with an employee who had dropped the ball on some tasks and whose behavior I perceived as insubordinate. During the meeting, she said some unkind things to me, and I melted down.

I, the one who had a reputation as a "cool cucumber," always calm under pressure, got up from my chair, burst into tears, made it to my supervisor's office, and told her I had to leave work. My words were, "I can't do this anymore." I gathered my purse from my office, hurried to my car, got in, and sped away. Coworkers were running behind my car in the parking lot, trying to stop me. This cool cucumber had created quite a bit of hot drama!

I drove across town at lightning speed. I'm surprised I wasn't stopped by the police. I wanted to get home quickly. I didn't have a plan for what I would do when I got home, but I needed to get away from the demands of life.

A police officer arrived at my house shortly after I did. I later learned that after I left work, one of my colleagues had called the police to go to my home for a welfare check. I wouldn't have answered the door, but I thought something may have happened to my daughter, so I answered. The kind police officer talked with me and tried to convince me that things would get better.

Through my tears, I told him they would not. He then convinced me to go with him to talk with someone. I got into the back of the police car because that's where one rides, even when not arrested for a crime. During the ride, still trying to be helpful, he suggested dietary changes and other strategies that might improve my depression.

When we arrived at the mental health facility and I attempted to get out of the car, I commented that since I'd never ridden in the back seat of a police car, I didn't know there were no door handles inside. He joked that it was for good reason. We chuckled.

Inside, I spoke with an intake counselor and let her know that life was overwhelming and I was tired. I was trying to find a reason to hang in and go on, but I couldn't seem to find one. We agreed that I would voluntarily spend a couple of days in the inpatient mental health facility. The first day and night, I cried continuously. I thought I would run out of tears.

I may have slept a bit as well. I declined any invitation to join others in the TV room or game room. I had no desire to eat. I got in trouble for letting other patients, who asked, eat my meals. Apparently, sharing food was not allowed. It was my first and only stay in a mental health facility. I broke that rule and several more, but others who were clearly repeat guests were quick to fill me in on how things worked.

I could write a few chapters about those days in the facility, but I will sum it up by saying that I had a couple of sessions with a psychiatrist and was released with a diagnosis of adjustment disorder and depression and a plan to reengage with my therapist. I complied.

I discussed and unpacked a lot as I resumed the sessions with my therapist. I recognized that during the two-year period leading up to my stay in the facility, I had experienced the death of my sister, the death of my mother, divorce, work-related stressors, church ministry stressors, selling a home, and buying a home as I transitioned between living situations. Those changes affected my well-being, and I had not adjusted well—hence my "adjustment disorder" diagnosis.

In addition to the two years of extreme stress, I had a longer-term pattern of failing to recognize when I needed to take care of myself. People close to me may have noticed that I needed a break to avoid a breakdown, but they didn't get involved or try to intervene. I may have been so good at hiding my depression and anxiety that no one noticed.

These days, I often hear the expression, "Check on your strong friends." My hope is that people are checking on their friends and family and not just repeating a cliché expression. It's important.

In the years since that incident, I have discovered joy and peace to replace depression and anxiety. Although I continue my relationship with my therapist. In addition to my family, I have a new community of colleagues and friends to support and encourage me. I know now that my life has value and purpose and that there is more for me to experience, accomplish, and enjoy.

God has worked behind the scenes as the Casting Director, unexpectedly removing people from my life—my sister, my mom, my first husband, work colleagues, and friends. Also, God sometimes unexpectedly puts people in place in my life. During the crisis period just described, he brought in the colleague who called the police, the police officer who conducted the welfare check, and the therapist who understands and helps me. God continues to ensure that family members, friends, business contacts, advisors, and people who simply care enough to encourage me are in the right place at the right time.

The Wrap Party / God as Production Manager

A Production Manager plans and hosts a post-production wrap party after a theater production ends. It is a time for celebration of accomplishments and looking toward the future. Guests and others who were not directly involved in the production are invited to share in the joy.

As I reflect on the experiences that I have shared in this chapter and look toward the future, I realize that I have a reason to celebrate. Each struggle prepared me for the next, making me wiser and stronger. My experiences were not just about me. I was chosen to endure them, celebrate overcoming them, and share my story so others may have hope.

Along the way, I have learned that my gifts, heart, personality, and experiences have been uniquely designed and orchestrated by God so that I have impact and influence in this world. My value and identity are not in the roles I may play as a wife, mother, sister, professional, friend, volunteer, or even a church ministry leader. I have an identity that reaches beyond any role.

Throughout my life, as I was making mistakes and wrong choices, doubting, hesitating, and being afraid, God was setting up new locations, new relationships, and new hope just for me. God is still working behind the scenes, setting the stage, creating the atmosphere, opening doors, and preparing for what comes next in my life. God has not finished writing my story, and as He gives me a more compelling testimony to help someone else, He uses me behind the scenes of someone else's story.

K.Renee Jenkins

Chapter 5

THE ROSE THAT GREW FROM GEORGIA CLAY: A TALE OF LETTING GO AND REDISCOVERY

I dedicate this to my mom. I know you would have been there for me every step of the way. However, this part of my journey I had to walk alone. I needed to know these were my choices, and mine alone.
I love you always.

As I unlocked my door, the numbness from the events that had happened earlier began to wear off, and I felt the emotions begin to flood in. *Keep it together, Carmen*, I told myself in an effort to hide the swelling in my eyes. I didn't want my daughter to get the slightest inkling that something was wrong with me.

As my daughter and her sister, who was staying with us for the weekend, walked through the door, I had only enough energy to walk straight to my bedroom and shut the door. I was thankful my bonus baby was there to keep my daughter entertained because otherwise, I didn't know how I was going to deal with what I was about to endure that weekend. I dropped my purse down onto a pile of clothes and grabbed my gold journal and the first pen I could find. I lay across my bed, opened my journal, and, without thought, I wrote, "A Letter to the One I Told to Stay." And there, all my emotions and words began to pour out . . .

Dear Baby,

I wanted you. I loved you already, and you hadn't even crossed over into this dimension yet. After all that has happened over these past few weeks, I still like to believe that you were made from love. Your father wasn't a man that meant nothing to me. I knew your father since I was eighteen years old, and, after years of being apart, our love and bond reconnected. However, in my mid to late thirties, I have come to see and learn that love isn't enough—not for two people to be together and make it work. But I will always love you.

I never knew I would be here writing such a letter, but here we are. I wanted you to know that as much as I wanted you and dreamt about you, I needed you to stay where you are cared for best. I didn't want you to cross over in this life and be met with trauma and an inherited generational curse. I didn't want you to grow up without your dad and have feelings of rejection, abandonment, and self-doubt.

You see, your dad had things going on—things that, to this day, I still don't understand. I'm not sure I will ever comprehend, but what I did come to understand is that he was not ready for you. He said he didn't want you. Even now, writing this letter hurts because how could he not want what was created out of love? How could he not want what we both used to dream and talk about? A son. You, my baby boy. I'm not even sure you would have even been a boy, but your dad and I would always say "son" whenever the subject of a kid came up. I was devastated to know he didn't want you, and even so, I thought I could still love you enough for the both of us.

I know in my heart that I could have made a way for you, and you would have been loved dearly by all those around you. But I felt in those quiet moments when no one was around, you would wonder, *Where is my dad?*, *Why didn't he want me?*, *Why did he have to die?*, or *Why is he in prison?* Those were the life paths your father gave me: death or prison. I was completely surprised by both, and I wanted you to deal with neither.

You see, we live in such a broken world—one that you could have made better, but I didn't want to risk it. I have seen what brokenness does to our men, especially our Black kings. The all too familiar storyline. The son the father didn't want or didn't care for. I saw the damage that can be done when a father willingly turns his back on his kids. The unwanted son was hurt, angry, and broken. He felt alone and abandoned. He felt as if something was wrong with him—why didn't his dad want him? He loved his other kids, so why not him? I didn't want you to feel like that. As healing as a mother's love can be, I still know how critical it is to have the love of a father, someone you love and trust to guide you through manhood. You deserved that, honestly and freely given. But to cross into this dimension, you wouldn't have had that with your dad.

Now, this isn't a letter to bash him because in my heart, I know he may have had his reasons, but I needed you to know why it's best to stay. Stay in glory, and fight for us on the other side. Remain in love and with God. I want more for you than what this world has to offer.

You see, my dear baby, to be born beautifully Black, you are already born into a lifetime disclaimer, even though this world was given to you to have dominion over. But the disclaimer is you would live, breathe, and understand that at times, others who don't look like you would disagree and dare to call and try to treat you less than. They would want to label you as trouble, and every day, you would have to keep that in mind—even as you walked home at night wearing your favorite hoodie and eating a bag of Skittles you just purchased from the corner store.

You would have to keep that in mind as you went for your daily run down the street, or when you simply pulled into a gas station with your favorite songs playing a bit loud. You would have to remember that disclaimer even as you played with a toy water gun in a park by our home, or if I ever needed you to go get your sister from a friend's house and you mistakenly went to the wrong address. I didn't want you to go through that on top of not having your dad around to be there for you.

I have so many thoughts running in my mind right now. *Am I making the right choice? Could I be wrong?* But I find comfort in knowing that I love you enough to say, "Don't come." Even as my body prepared a place for you to grow, "Don't come." Stay in perfect peace. Stay in love and with our Father in Heaven. Stay where your spirit can live infinitely and not be subjected to the cruelness of this world. Stay in the high places that I can only dream of for now, and one day, I can meet you and know you, and you know me also.

The pain I feel is like no other. Please forgive me, my love . . . my baby.

There will be a place one day that you and I can meet, and I hope to know you. A meeting of familiar souls. I hope you know that I love you now, and I will love you then. I hope my love stretches through all dimensions and multiverses. I cry for you. I cry because I will not get to hold you and kiss you in this lifetime. I cry because I won't see you with your sister in this lifetime. This hurts so bad, my dear baby, but I feel and know this is best. As selfish as I want to be by keeping you here, I also know it is not just about me and my wants.

Our time together was short, but it will live with me forever. I love you so much, and I ask God to comfort me in your physical absence. You weren't a mistake to me. You have taught me so much already. You taught me to consider your emotional future in a way that would impact generations. It's sad, but our Black men aren't

121

taught to deal with their emotions very well, and if I'm being fully transparent, there are not a lot of safe spaces for them to express those emotions and feelings.

I wanted you to have that safe space for you in your father, not just me. I know some people would say the man God has for me would be able to show you the love you never got from your birth father. However, I have seen that however close it can come, it is never quite the same.

I don't know how it would have been. I was told you would be fatherless, and I had to really consider that. It is the only reason I was considering breaking a promise I made to God.

Was my selfish love to want you to stay going to cost you more in the end? I didn't want to risk it. Broken families have been the demise of our people, son. It must stop.

You deserved a whole and healed family, but that would not have been our reality. So, please know that my love for you is one that liberates. I love you too much to let you go, but I love you more to tell you to stay. I love you now, and I will love you then.

Love Always,

Mommy

As I closed my journal and ended my letter, I then took the final set of pills to complete my medical abortion. Alone in my room, feeling everything from grief to anger to despair, I thought to myself, *How did I get here . . . again? After all this "healing" I've done, how did I manage to get to this point? After surviving narcissistic, abusive relationships, how did I get here? After ridding myself of toxic relationships and ending a marriage, how did I end up here? . . . Again?*

These were all the questions I had racing in my mind, yet I had no time to process any of them because I was enduring the pain of going through a voluntary miscarriage at home. At first, all I could feel were the cramps, yet these were the cramps you didn't want to feel being pregnant because you knew what was tragically coming next. I felt horrible inside because as a woman, I love the magic of our feminine bodies. We hold the space to harvest and push life into this world, yet I was giving mine back.

I feared judgment from those who would disagree with my choices and call me all sorts of names without hearing my story or my why. In hindsight, the opinions of strangers or those who don't know me should have never been a fear of mine. But I digress.

That whole weekend, I don't think I spoke many words. All that I could say was found in my tear-stained gold journal. I had a series of contradictory feelings coming in like waves crashing on the shore in the midst of a hurricane. One minute, I was at peace with my decision, and the next, I wondered if I made a mistake. One minute, I felt like I made the best decision for me and my never-to-be-born child; the next minute, I wondered if I could have really been a single parent two times over. I was all over the place, honestly. But in my heart, I knew I made the right decision, and I just had to endure this part of the journey.

As the weekend passed, and the weeks continued to come, I found strength in the very words I wrote in my letter. Week after week, I found solace in my choice to leave my baby with God. I saw what we were both being protected from. I saw how my choice protected the lives of my family and anyone new to come into my life. I saw how we were saved from being pulled into the misery and destruction of what wasn't supposed to be, and I was thankful.

However, as thankful as I was, I told myself that work within myself still needed to be done. I needed to look within myself to understand the decisions I made and connect the dots between all of my life's blows to understand the why. *Why is all of this happening? What is God truly trying to tell me in this collection of seasons I have endured for the past eleven years? What within me do I need to change to experience better?*

Not many people knew what I was going through at that time—not even my own mother. She always calls me the queen of secrets, but it has always been my way to go into my shell and endure my trials alone. Only a select few knew that at the same time I was enduring the pain of losing my baby, I was also four months into yet another layoff. At one point, I experienced four layoffs within three years, and the second layoff happened when I found out I was pregnant with my now nine-year-old daughter. I spent that time unemployed, depressed, pregnant, and alone, struggling to understand why God was allowing all this to happen to me. I felt abandoned and rejected.

Love—or, should I say, the need and want for love—can land you in some compromising situations that only God can deliver you from. That same desire for love can keep you in abusive relationships that cause you to question yourself and your sanity.

That longing for love can have you entangled with people and ideologies that only push you further from God, yourself, and those closest to you.

But that was the lesson, or level of understanding, God was bringing me to amid all of the trials and tribulations I endured. It wasn't about those who I felt didn't love and treat me the way I needed and wanted. Nope. The very love and treatment I was searching for rested within Him and within the very woman I was looking at in the mirror. And that was my journey: one of self-love, self-rediscovery, grace, forgiveness, and redefining self-confidence.

What Is Self-Love?

Some people would define self-love as weekly spa days and solo dates, while others would say self-love is being in perfect physical shape while having a fly wardrobe and a fancy car that you bought to display on social media. To me, self-love looks like being able to ask yourself the hard questions of why you are the way you are in an effort to become the best version of yourself; being able to look in the mirror and call out the good, bad, and severely ugly parts of yourself, then put in the hard work to fix those things within.

Self-love is being able to look at all the choices you have made in your life, look at all the moments that brought you to your knees in despair, and own them. Own them in a way that no longer gives them an emotional hold but in a way to say, "Yes, this happened; yes, I went through that; but in the end, I can truly say I love myself because I overcame it all. I love who it made me become."

It doesn't matter if I had to crawl through it or get carried through it—I made it through. All that I endured made me into who I am. I survived what has killed others, and in the end, I'm rocking with me if no one else is. I love myself because I am battle tested, and I know I am more than a conqueror.

Self-love is taking the necessary steps to just be better and appreciate all that you are and who God called you to be. Self-love is realizing that all parts are needed in this journey to love. The good cannot be fully appreciated without knowing and experiencing the bad. It is the bad times, the trials, and the pain that teach us life's greatest lessons. It shows us who we truly are in the face of adversity, and, hopefully, it teaches us to look within and gauge our own self-awareness.

My search for self-love made me realize that I have always been enough. I have always been worthy to receive love, even when I felt like I didn't deserve it. God needed me to get to that point—I had to believe that on my own and not have it validated through the love of others. I needed to see and understand my worth and how it exceeded the price of rubies. I had to look at the very moments in my life and say it wasn't all happening *to* me, it was happening *for* me. It was happening for me to be pruned so I could grow and learn; it was only putting me in a better position to receive the very desires of my own heart. I just needed to realign those desires.

To me, self-love looks like standing in the mirror, looking at yourself from the inside out, and saying, "I love who you are. I love the mindset I have, and who I am at the core. Even if I have things that I want to change within myself, I love how I will never stop trying to achieve my goals. I'm proud of how I handle the lemons I receive in life."

I have learned to love being confident in who I am as a woman and as a person. I love how I can show up unapologetically me and no longer feel the need to shrink. I'm taking up space again. So, even if I see things I want to change on the outside, I know my worth is not defined by it.

Redefining Self-Confidence

For the longest, my self-love was measured by how I viewed myself physically. Self-love and self-confidence became synonymous in my eyes. I felt that it was easier to love myself if I liked how I looked. However, in my case, I struggled with self-image issues for a very long time. So, I didn't have very high self-esteem, even though most people assumed I did. Most were surprised to learn that about me.

Then, in 2017, something clicked, and I completely transformed my body by losing seventy pounds. I truly shocked myself because I did not think I was capable of doing that. A lot of people asked me what all I did to lose the weight, and the answer was not what most expected to hear: "When I decided to shed my emotional weight, the body simply followed."

At the time, every day was a gift to me to be better. I challenged and pushed myself mentally by reading more. I put hours in at the gym consistently, and I spent time with God and gained so much insight and wisdom. I was so happy and proud of how I looked and felt. But even then, I didn't know that I still had some deeper things I was going to have to endure just around the corner.

Shortly after my one-year mark of consistency and weight loss, some deep memories came to the surface for me. I remember crying while telling my story to someone close about a group of boys that attempted to sexually assault me in the fifth grade. It happened so long ago, and it was something I didn't talk about, so it shocked me when I cried talking about it at that moment. I realized then that I would have to go back and heal the inner child and teenager within myself, no matter how much I weighed.

That wouldn't be the last time I was forced to face some painful moments in my life. By 2019, I had finally made the decision to end my marriage, and during the COVID-19 pandemic, I was filing for divorce and starting completely over. That was a time when I felt stretched the most because my divorce was only a portion of everything I had going on.

I wasn't happy at my job anymore, and working during COVID-19 while my daughter was in virtual school was a tough transition. At the same time, relationships that meant the world to me were being challenged, and by the end of 2020, I was mentally exhausted. It was a lot to unpack, and slowly, I began to move further away from who I was back in 2017.

I became so hard on myself for doing so that I punished myself even more by becoming a recluse and continuing to emotionally eat. Slowly, my self-confidence began to dwindle, and my self-love followed. I would continue to struggle with this for the next couple of years.

But then, I remember praying, asking God to help me restore my viewpoint of myself. I just got tired (again) of feeling bad about myself. Sure, I had things I wanted to change, but I was no longer going to postpone my happiness until I made those changes. I decided I was going to be happy along the way and love on myself at every stage of my journey.

I began to ask myself, *Why do I have low self-esteem?*, and everything that came back was, in my eyes, very surface-level. I began to challenge my own thoughts by saying, *Yeah, I may not like this, but I do like this, that, and the third.* The more I did that, the more I realized I had been lying to myself. It wasn't that I didn't love myself; I just focused on the things I didn't like about myself instead of appreciating and strengthening the things I did love.

I found confidence within myself when I realized I am enough as is. I am confident in who I am as a person. I remain authentic to who I am, and I love being surrounded by people who feel the same about themselves. I look at different time periods in my life, and I see just how far I have come. It didn't matter how ugly the road may have gotten at times; I still chose to show up. Realizing that showed me that I was giving my faults too much spotlight.

And so, I redefined what confidence was for me. It's not about how you look or the things you own. It's about who you are on the inside—your character, your heart, and your spirit. I asked myself, *If those things were all you had to your name, would you be confident in yourself?*

Are you confident in how you treat others and how you care for them? Can you show up for them in the ways that matter most? Are you confident in how you are raising your daughter? Can you be proud of what you are showing her and teaching her?

When I thought that way, I realized I was answering yes more than no. If I did have a no, I was confident that I would make the effort to change it and be better. In essence, I learned to take it easy and stop being so hard on myself. That was a game-changer.

Redefining Self-Confidence: When Favor Showed Up

It was the end of 2020, and I was just tired. I was tired in every way possible. My daughter and I were still living with my mother and stepdad in the upstairs den as I worked to purchase my first home. I was doing everything right to get this house, and then, *boom*—my truck died. Out of nowhere. It was December 30, and that was the last news I needed. At that point, I was so used to getting unwanted news that all I could do was laugh and thank God it wasn't anything worse. I didn't want to go home so quickly feeling like crap, so I went to the house of my dear friend, whom I love like a sister. By the time I got to her house, she already had her stepdad on the phone to assist me with getting a car. My situation didn't look so great since I owed on my last vehicle. Even the rep at the dealership said it didn't look good for me. I thought I was going home with a Ford Focus—but God. Within one business day, I was in a brand new 2020 SUV. By January, my divorce was final, and by February, I was moving into my first apartment—a brand new complex and unit—after having to sleep on a sofa bed for two years. By the end of April, I was offered a new position at an amazing company. God literally told me, "Everything will be new." Even my title within my career changed. God told me—and showed me—"No matter what the situation may look like, I'm here." And, just like God, He blessed me in His fashion. It was almost like He was waiting for my situation to look impossible before He came in and said, "It is so." Favor.

Saying Goodbye to the Former Version of Me

A part of not being so hard on myself was learning to say goodbye to the old versions of myself. Sometimes, the hardest soul tie you will ever have to break is the one you have with your former self. That can be extremely difficult because as you evolve in life, you will be required to make tough decisions and tough choices.

You will be called to let things go, you will have to let things pass, and you will have to move on. Sometimes, that means moving on from people; sometimes, it's a relationship or even marriage. It could even be the very things within yourself that you formed as a self-defense mechanism in order to survive your former circumstances.

Maybe you were guarded and closed off because you were in a situation that required you to numb your feelings to avoid conflict. But now, this season of your life requires you to be open and vulnerable. Maybe before, you had to dim your light so that those closest around you didn't feel as though you were outshining them, but now, this new season is calling you to stretch with boldness.

By not letting go of the former things, you can hold yourself back from the new places you are being called to. It can hold you back from meeting your new tribe of people who are meant to be a part of this next phase of your life. Change is never easy, but as they say, your new life will always cost you the old one.

As I mentioned before, 2017 was somewhat of a golden year for me. Whenever I would meditate, I would record voice memos of the downloads I would get in my moments with God. It was a time when I really experienced the fruit of the Spirit, so I have dozens of notes.

I had never felt so aligned, and so, it became the standard of how I felt I needed to be. When I felt myself falling off, I tried my best to get back to the version of myself that I was in 2017. That was a big mistake because I struggled so badly trying to do that.

Recently, I found myself listening to the recordings I created during that time. I listened to what I was saying. I was so full of hope and still trying to speak life into dead situations. Yes, I was transforming my life, but the Carmen in those recordings hadn't faced her divorce yet. I realized the version of myself I was trying to get back to didn't exist anymore.

I listened to the things I was saying, and the woman I am today would have interjected and told myself to let go of the thing I was holding on to tightest. I would have told her that she had her answer back then; she just didn't want to accept it. I would have told her that although she was on the right track, she still had more to learn. The woman I am today has gained so much more knowledge. So, it was time to let that 2017 version of Carmen go once and for all because she didn't meet the new minimum qualifications of this level in my life.

This was a challenge to me because I didn't know just how deeply connected I was to my former self. Oftentimes, we can be scared to go through such a process because it doesn't always look like unicorns and rainbows. It can look like a dark shelf cloud that has no ending in sight.

It can look like torrential rain downpours. It can sometimes feel like isolation and loneliness. It can feel like you are all over the place emotionally, where you are happy today and can't get out of bed tomorrow. I had to accept that the old has been out, so I should appreciate the new. It would take time to do this, but giving yourself grace is a part of self-love.

It's Layers to This: Grace, That Is

Recently, I learned that a component of self-love looks like giving yourself grace to grow through and forgive the choices you made without full understanding. Grace is being able to say, "I did the best I could with what I knew at the time," and finding peace with seeing the wisdom in hindsight.

It was storming the other day, and, as I do during most storms, I sat out on my balcony and viewed the storms from a distance. I have seen the sky change through so many beautiful colors since my time in my home. I have seen streaks of purple mixed with various shades of orange. I have seen soft baby blue hues mixed with blush pink clouds from the sunset.

But this particular day, as I was sitting on the sofa in my living room, drafting this very chapter, I noticed a dark change in skylight. I went out to the balcony, and I immediately saw an extremely dark gray cloud passing right over my apartment building. It was a massive shelf cloud that stretched across my entire line of sight.

I noticed how layered the clouds were towards the tail end of this huge shelf. It was pretty windy, and I could see how the lower clouds were dark, yet moving fast. I then looked closer and saw that the higher clouds seemed to not be moving at all. It made me think about previous flights I have taken, where it was storming in Atlanta, but as soon as we ascended to a certain height, we were no longer in the storm, and all was sunny and bright outside.

I thought to myself, *While I'm being hard on myself, grace is telling me it is levels to this. The same way the pilot on those flights had to fly through it to get above and over it is the same you will have to do for yourself. You will have to give yourself grace to slowly rise through the darkest of clouds until you get above and over it to see the sunlight and clear skies.*

God told me perfection was never the requirement. He wasn't looking for a perfect ten performance every time. He knew I would make the choices I would and go through the things I did. So, why would He be upset about what He already knew?

It was a semi-epiphany to me. When God still blessed me despite my failures, I saw just how gentle He was with me. For so long, I had experienced the harshness of others; I internally received God to be the same way. But He showed me otherwise.

134

What I didn't realize was that as I gave myself grace, I was also opening the door for all my emotions to come up and come out, and there, I found anger.

Yes, I Am a Mad Black Woman . . . And That's Okay

As a bBack woman, it is extremely common for us to be given the "angry Black woman" label. Tyler Perry even titled one of his films that, *Diary of a Mad Black Woman*. The problem is that label infuriates us as Black women.

Why? Because it is a statement that carries an assumption that Black women are always mad about something. We get labeled as aggressive or too masculine, and because of it, some men prefer not to date us.

The reality is, that statement takes away a woman's right to be just that: mad—so much so that a Black woman may overcompensate her niceness to avoid getting labeled as the "aggressive, mad Black woman." I found myself doing this early in my career in corporate America.

I was around different cultures who didn't know how to receive a tall, five feet eleven inches tall, and full-figured Black woman with a Type A personality. So, I often found myself smiling a little harder than normal while in the office. Now, thirteen years into my career, I no longer feel the need to do that.

The crazy thing is, even as a Type A personality, I was very passive in my actual relationships. I didn't want to get labeled as a nagger or argumentative. In the end, it only caused me to bottle up my real emotions, and, slowly, I began to implode. In relationships, whether romantic or not, sometimes, I would avoid speaking on certain feelings I had to avoid confrontation.

Confrontation was something I genuinely disliked, but I learned that when you suppress your emotions to prevent discomfort within someone else, it only increases the discomfort within yourself. And, eventually, it all comes out. For me, I didn't want to admit I was angry. I didn't want to verbalize that. I wanted to believe that I could pass over that part and move straight into the kumbaya phase. Negative.

After everything I went through—family drama and trauma, sexual assault, narcissistic abuse, abandonment, a toxic marriage, and financial hardship—yeah, I was mad. I was mad I went through all that. I was mad at those who hurt me. I was mad at those who left me when I needed them most. I was mad at how ending my marriage ended several relationships that I thought would last a lifetime.

But, above all of that, I was mad at the version of myself that had accepted certain things that this version of me would never. I was mad at my former self for tolerating disrespect for the sake of keeping a relationship. I was mad at how I allowed myself to dim my light so that others could feel comfortable. I was mad that my self-esteem and self-worth were so low that I entertained people I had no business being around. I felt all of this, yet I was trying to mask it all in my everyday life. But enough was enough.

One day, I was talking to a really good friend of mine, and I told her, "You know what? I am mad."

Her response to me was, "And it's okay to be mad. Just don't stay there."

At that moment, I gave myself permission to feel my anger. By doing so, it allowed that emotion to come up and pass. Once my anger passed, the strategy followed. I was able to acknowledge my anger and then unpack it so it would no longer hold me back.

As Black women, it's okay to be mad. We are human, the same as everyone else, and we all share the same emotions. The reasons may vary, but we hurt the same.

A part of me redefining my definition of self-love and confidence was accepting this concept. I love me enough to allow myself to honestly feel my emotions. I could no longer allow my hurt and anger to take up any more space inside me.

Unhealed hurt and anger only collect interest over the years, and I was maxing out. Once I finally acknowledged all my emotions, I began to let them go and redirect that energy into healing from my past.

Forgiveness Is Essential to the Soul

It has not been easy getting to this place of reaching beyond my comfort, stepping into this new version of myself, and forgiving the old me. It has not been easy forgiving those who never asked for it in the first place. But as I have been on this journey of redefining my confidence and discovering this version of me with grace there to assist me, I must also learn to extend the same grace to others.

I had to learn to forgive the old version of me, and so I had to learn to forgive the version of others that may have hurt me. When I compare 2017 to 2023, I can say that I was dealing with very different issues during both time periods. So, anyone who may have known me during each of those times may have a different perspective of me.

The same applies to anyone else I have crossed paths with in life. Maybe the version of who they were then is not the same as who they are today. Maybe they stayed the same. All I know is that whichever version I received was the one that was needed for that part of my life.

When I began to look at it that way, forgiveness become a bit easier. In our interpersonal interactions, we serve as the versions of ourselves that are most needed by others. Some versions come to teach; others come to transform. I can't hold on to the specifics of what someone has done because it can take over what I am supposed to learn.

Instead of focusing on the pain a person caused me, I focused on the perspective that this person was just a vessel used to get me to move according to God's will. When I released myself from the emotional bondage of pain and hurt and extended forgiveness, I released so much emotional weight and baggage that was holding me down. I finally felt lighter.

I Said All That to Say . . .

Everyone's journey in life is different, and it is personal. By nature, I am a very private person, so the fact that I am even sharing my story along with eleven other amazing women, is a huge leap outside of my comfort zone. But I love it! It's the scariest and most beautiful feeling.

It is the leaps like this, paired with a committed mind and a surrendered soul, that make this journey beautiful. It is breathtaking to see yourself transform into the person you daydream about. It gives you strength to know that when the hard times come, you come out on top every time, even if you take a lick or two. You know how to handle the trenches if you ever have to go back there.

As I continue to grow and evolve, I learn how critical it is to leave old ways behind in order to advance to the next level. At times, the goodbyes have been hard and painful, but in the end, I have gained more confidence in myself, knowing that when I am faced with tough decisions, I am willing to make the right choice, even if it hurts.

During my darkest seasons, God always assigned select people in my life to give me words of encouragement when I needed it most. This has been my favor. I'm sharing my story—one that is personal, one that is dear to me, and one that is still being written. Some of these moments in my life were hard to share publicly. I was very raw in my emotions and thoughts, and I just let my pen take off.

While writing, I didn't care about who would think what. I expressed my thoughts freely. My hopes are for the ones who see themselves in my moments, that they can also see what it feels like to be on the other side of the hurt or the tough season.

There were certain moments that caused me to stop and really think about my next steps. What did I want for myself in all areas of my life? There were moments when I truly had to look within and decide to do the work. You cannot escape the work. It was not always easy because you must be real with yourself, and sometimes, you have to revisit the past to make peace with it so you can move on.

As hard as it was, is, and can be, it will always be worth it. When you leave the old behind, you get excited about what's to come. A new territory, a new level, has been unlocked. By dealing with your hurts and pains and clearing them out, you finally make space for God to pour something new into your life. And guess what . . . It's always BIGGER.

I titled my chapter "The Rose That Grew from Georgia Clay," not just as a way to pay homage to my Georgian roots or show tribute to Tupac's "A Rose That Grew from Concrete." I chose this title because it was my way of describing how something beautiful can grow through muddy clay, a place where you wouldn't expect a rose to grow and thrive. However, it wasn't until I actually began to research the growing conditions of roses in red clay that it all really came together.

Based on my collection of research, I learned that it is possible for a rose to grow in clay soil. However, the best way to support the growth in that same clay soil was by adding organic compost. When I looked at what organic compost consisted of , it included old fruits, vegetables, bark chippings, and even manure. So, a bit of everything can be found in this organic compost. How poetic is that? If we symbolize the rose, then that means everything we have gone through and have consumed becomes our compost. Our trials, tribulations, and tough seasons—or manure, if you will—all contributed to the richness of the very soil we needed to grow in.

In my eyes, that is favor: God taking everything you have endured—the good, bad, and even unspeakable parts—and using all to make you richer. Even when the conditions seem to not permit greatness or success, God opens a window and says, "It is so."

This anthology is one that talks about phenomenal favor. Sure, I could write about all the miraculous moments when God showed up in my life, but I also found favor in the small moments while I was going through my darkest of hours. I found favor when something was deeply troubling my heart, and I hadn't even used my words to talk to God about it—yet, before I closed my eyes for the night, answers were given.

I have seen God's favor when He comes in clutch like Kobe Bryant during the NBA Championship Finals. God has truly favored me, and whenever I felt lonely, He always let me know He was right there.

But the greatest favor of them all is the favor I found in the grace that God granted me to simply become. And that is phenomenal.

Carmen Aerise

143

Chapter 6

FAVOR THROUGHOUT

This chapter is dedicated to my son, "Trey." You are indeed my greatest accomplishment. May you always lead with love, may you know joy, and may you always shine your beautiful light, especially in the darkness.

You, my son, are God's best.

The realization of self has little to do with what you've done, in comparison to being fully open to God's grace and plan for your life. For me, it has always been God's grace and mercy that followed me throughout my life that have made me the person that I am today. Flaws and all, God has called me, as He has you, to be in alignment with our divine purpose. Listen to that little voice inside yourself, pray, seek God's counsel, and be prepared for the unexpected.

Whoen you are the oldest daughter and the eldest of six grandchildren, the unspoken pressure is always on. That little voice telling you, "Someone's watching you

. . . set the standard . . . do the right thing," never quite goes away. Ever since I could remember, all I did was the right thing—or, at least that's what I thought. I was a private-school-educated, Sunday-school-goin', extracurricular-participating, multi-sport-playing, fun-loving girl.

I did all the things "they" said you do in order to sustain a life worth living. A life that a young lady, brought up like myself, strives for. You know, go to school, get a good education, find a man, get married, have a family. All the things that I—yes, I—wanted, and of course, all the things that my family wanted. However, as I got older, I realized that this life—MY LIFE—was about more than what people wanted for me, and, even more than what I wanted for myself.

Upon graduating from college, I knew that I wanted to have a career in business marketing. My plan was to live in Washington, D.C., for one year; live in New York City for a year following that; and go to Los Angeles for a year before ultimately settling on the east coast. I was twenty-four years old, single, and had no children—it was the perfect plan. But you know what they say: If you want to make God laugh, tell Him your plans.

It was 2012, and I was so excited to be fulfilling my goal of moving to D.C.—in the Obama years, at that. There was a special kind of thrill that came with turning the door knob of my own apartment, buying my first set of furniture, moving to a place where I only knew three people, and landing my first real job. I would wake up every morning and catch the private shuttle in my neighborhood to the train. Or, if I was running behind, I would jump in my new Nissan Sentra, and hustle through the traffic to my office in Midtown (three blocks from the White House). At that time, my car was the biggest purchase that I had ever made. However, on this particular morning, when I ran out of my apartment in my business casual, as professional recruiters do, I looked around, and my car was GONE!

After a bit of a panic, reality began setting in: Partying three times a week, attempting to keep up with friends, juggling work, and promising myself that I wouldn't ask family for help had all caught up with me.

Your car's been repossessed, I hesitantly, yet firmly, told myself.

Between the painful pounding in my chest and the mere thought of the disappointment of my family, I knew that this was something that would change everything.

It was March 2013, and my parents, alongside my grandparents ("Mama and Papa") drove two hours to my apartment to have a talk with me face-to-face.

"Jasmine," Papa started, in that voice that only grandfathers have (he was also the cosigner, as I hadn't had much credit history yet). "I will help you out of this, but this cannot happen again. We [as he clearly spoke for the collective] will pay the money to get your car back."

But before he could finish, my mom would interject with, " . . . But we all think that you need to come home!"

That was probably one of the worst days of my life. Here I was, a twenty-five-year-old adult, being TOLD to come back home.

After being there for about two hours, my family left my apartment and drove back home. I remember sitting in my little living room, which doubled as a dining area, a quaint space that I was so proud of—my first apartment as a young professional. It may have been small, it may have even been a bit dated, but it was mine. But suddenly, none of that mattered. *So, what now? I leave my job and this new place that I call home, and, to add insult to injury, move back home?!* I couldn't bear the thought.

Two months later, on Memorial Day weekend, I moved back to the Hampton Roads area of Virginia. This is the moment in which God got His laugh. Virginia wasn't my true home, as I was born and raised in Connecticut. However, after my grandparents left Connecticut in '99 to retire in Chesapeake, Virginia, my parents later followed them the summer before my sophomore year at Hampton University. My plan was to go home and save money, which was the problem from the very beginning. Once I did that, I would continue with my plan to New York and Los Angeles.

During my time at home, I did a lot of soul-searching. I began going back to church on a regular basis (as I had all my life, prior to college) and hanging out with friends from Hampton who were still in the area, and, in that, a relationship was formed between myself and someone whom I knew since I was an eighteen-year-old freshman: Troy. I met Troy through friends; he hung with a group of about ten guys, and my circle had seven.

We were in the same class, and, ironically, we both changed our majors to pursue a business degree, where we found ourselves doing two group projects together. However, he and I never hung out; as a matter of fact, the day he kicked me out of his apartment for being sick in the bathroom during a party his roommates had while he was at work, I knew we would never be friends. I guess the joke was on me.

Relationships are not the easiest thing in the world, but when Troy and I got together, we knew each other. Our comfortability had already been established, which created a safe space where things just felt right. We would spend days on end together for six months, not realizing the trajectory that we were on until one day in May 2014. The day we found out that we would be expecting our first child together.

God laughed.

At the time of the news, I was so happy, but Troy's fear of the unknown considering the newness of our relationship dimmed my excitement. Although both of our parents are married, Troy and I were both born out of wedlock, and our parents went on to marry other people. He didn't want that for us, and I respected that, but that became more of a stressor than a motivator. Stress mounted, but all along, I knew that despite our sin, God would create a path for us and our child that would serve us well and, most importantly, serve Him. It was during those early days that I realized my faith would have to carry both me and Troy.

I had been working in human resources at a Fortune 500 company for about a year and a half when I found out that I was pregnant, and, thankfully, my job was extremely "cushiony." Upon completion of a major benefit buyout project, my diligence (I worked extended hours) and professionalism proved myself worthy of non-micromanagement. Thank God!

So, instead of being on the phone with customers and dealing with pensions, death benefits, severance packages, and more buyouts, my manager, Maria, allowed me to receive the same pay for a fraction of the work. I would think to myself all the time, while doing my minimal job of checking fax machines for personal identification information and taking calls at the front desk, *How do pregnant women go to work every day?*

When I wasn't at the front desk, checking fax machines, or eating the six-pack of peanut butter crackers from the vending machine, I was sitting in a cubicle, struggling to keep my eyes open. It should be against the law for anyone pregnant to work unless they choose to. The changes that our bodies undergo, though amazing and filled with wonderment, are also taxing, fragile, and beyond exhausting. My friend, Kim, was a lifesaver during those days when I struggled most, especially during my second trimester.

She'd whisper as loudly as she could, "Jasmine, wake up! Someone's coming!"

I would jolt myself awake! . . . causing that tight, gut-wrenching feeling you get when you wake up in a panic because you weren't supposed to fall asleep in the first place. It's terrible, and it feels ten times worse when a little person is growing inside of you. If I could have stopped working I would have, but at that time, I didn't have that luxury. But through it all, I was able to see God's hand on my life. Maria was His vessel; she showed me favor, setting me apart from the others, and she gave me what I didn't even know I would need in the future: a space where I could be at rest mentally and physically.

The days turned into weeks, and weeks into months. Before I knew it, I was in my third trimester, fifty-three pounds heavier. It was as if everything was moving at the speed of light. Everything was changing . . . I was changing—not only physically but also mentally, spiritually, and most definitely emotionally. I was nervous. I was scared. I was overjoyed. I was anxious, but overall, I kept telling myself, *You're going to be a mother!* A great mother—one like my own mother and grandmother, strong women of value, intelligence, and integrity.

The homefront was touch and go. Although Troy and I were excited for the baby to come, we were also two unmarried people in our twenties attempting to create a life together. There's something to be said about waiting to have a child until after marriage. That, of course, was always my plan, but we made a choice to move forward with the decisions that we had made. I truly wished that we had the security, the covering, and the sanctity of marriage. On one hand, we both knew that we loved each other very much. On the other hand, we knew that if the other one wanted to walk away, there wouldn't be much that we could do to stop it, and that's where the frustration came from—at least, for me. Now, looking back, I'm glad that Troy never left me and I never left Troy; we stuck it out, we prayed, and we hoped for all good things, even when we couldn't see them.

Since I was due to have our son on February 8, my last day for work was scheduled for February 6. That day, I walked in, and my desk was covered in balloons, cards, and well wishes for a healthy and safe delivery. I was overwhelmed with emotion. It finally hit me that I would be leaving a space where I went daily to make a living to go and create my own space and a new "living." A safe place for my child to live, grow, learn, laugh, cry, and dream, with myself and Troy comanaging and using resources we had not just financially but spiritually. That's how we would "make a living."

All my life, I wanted to be a mother. I remember knowing beyond a shadow of a doubt that I would have a son. There was no question in my mind. God told me this, and He later revealed it in a dream. During my pregnancy, I dreamt of my son laying in his crib. All I could see was the back of him; his little, light blue baby pants; and the classic white onesie that every baby has worn.

February 8 came, but the baby wasn't ready. So, we went to church, and after, Troy and I went out to lunch. I took a picture outside near a beautiful tree because I wanted to commemorate the date that the doctors said Trey would come. When we looked at the picture, there was a long, wide, golden streak that seemed to shoot across the lush green tree that I stood next to. It was clearly a ray from the bright sun that day, but this ray of sunlight was something that neither Troy nor I had ever seen captured in a picture. It directly touched my stomach—no other part of my body. It was the most beautiful sign from God, reassuring us that our baby was okay and, most importantly, protected. That picture made it clear to me that I was carrying a special child.

Perhaps I needed that reassurance because on February 10 at 5:00 p.m., I was rushed into an operation room after being in labor for seventeen hours, but I hadn't dilated more than seven centimeters. In order to have a natural delivery, a woman must be at ten centimeters, but for whatever reason, my body would not go past this threshold.

"Jasmine, we have to get you in the OR because the baby's heart rate is going down . . . I'm going to have to do an emergency C-section," my doctor insisted.

I don't remember what she said after that. All I could think about was seeing my child's face, seeing my child . . . alive. I was given even more drugs than I was already on, which, in hindsight, may have been for the best so that I didn't simply lay there and cry the entire time. Everything happened so fast; it was as if I teleported to the operating room.

The room was cold, empty, and blindingly white all around, very similar to something you'd see in a dream. There were about five doctors all circled around me. Troy was at the top right side of the bed while the doctors remained beyond the blue mini curtain that censored whatever it was that they were doing to me. I couldn't feel a thing; the deliriousness from the drugs had me cracking jokes the entire procedure, something I definitely would not have done if I had been in my right mind.

By God's grace, my son, Troy III ("Trey"), was born that evening at 5:59 p.m. I saw his face; I heard his cry. All was well, and my life began all over again.

After being in the hospital for three days, we returned home, and two months later, I returned to work. Things at work felt different. I couldn't quite put my finger on what it was, but I felt change a-coming. Prior to leaving for maternity leave, I went back to doing benefits over the phone, so the "cushy" part was a thing of the past. I saw it as earning my stripes as a working mom, and I earned every single stripe.

I was getting used to my new routine of having a child at daycare while working forty-five minutes away from home, picking up the baby, coming home exhausted, and still having to breastfeed the baby and cook for Troy, who didn't get home from work until 11 p.m. Troy worked a rotating schedule at that time, which was extremely taxing the first five years of parenthood. When I was leaving, he was just waking up, and when he was coming home, I was heading to bed. Between work, a new baby, new bills, and our opposite schedules, we were tired, stressed, and irritable.

Almost inevitably, the affection began to lack, and the frustration began to mount. We needed to figure out the "us" part—where did *we* fit now? At that time, the baby and our jobs seemed to be all that we had time for. Weekends were never long enough, and although we had help from my family, we knew that this was our responsibility; therefore, we never abused our support system or took it for granted.

Our saving grace was that our son was the best baby. It was as if he knew that we needed him to fit into our lives as easily as possible, and he did. What felt like imbalance was truly the beginning of alignment for our little family. Our son was our blessing.

One Monday, a month after returning back to work, I found out that my manager, Maria, had been fired. They let her go with no forewarning, and not one meeting was held to share the news with her teams. I was devastated. It took a while, but I found her personal Facebook page; I couldn't let her leave without thanking her for all she had done for me. I would later realize that she was part of the reason that I chose to stay on the job for as long as I had and that this was simply God "shaking the tree."

Within a month, new management came in. In addition to receiving a new manager, the company also replaced the director, with whom I also had a great rapport.

I'll never forget the day that I was sitting at the front desk (which I still did for a few hours a day), and I was casually introduced to the new director. Yet again, there had been no formal meetings pertaining to the hiring of my new manager or the new director. She came downstairs and around from the right side of the front desk, slowly walking, finally meeting me and my coworker, Ms. Lori, face-to-face. I was surprised to find that she, too, was a woman of color and only about three years my senior.

Ms. Lori introduced us. "Jasmine, this is Tonia, our new director."

"Nice to meet you," I said smiling.

For some reason, that was all that I could muster up. I'm usually a "chatty Cathy," but not that day. In hindsight, her spirit was off from the beginning. I always try to see the good in people, especially when I first meet them, so it was hard for me to see her for who she truly was at that time. She went on to tell us that she had moved from out of state and was still living in a hotel, looking for a permanent apartment. Since I knew the area pretty well, I emailed her a few places that I thought she might like.

As the days went on, things began to change. Quietly, she was, as my mother puts it, "cleaning house." Daily, she would walk up and down the rows of cubicles with a condescending smile, inquiring about the job or our families or just making friendly small talk, but behind closed doors, she was wreaking havoc. It didn't take long for word to get around the office that she was mainly firing women. Out of nearly forty people she terminated, some of which were my friends, less than ten were men. Based on the very specific people she chose to let go, it was a shared conception that she was releasing those whom she felt threatened by.

The majority of these women were high performers on the job, physically attractive, or a combination of the two. It was at that point that I made the decision to keep all conversation at a business level. There was hardly ever any outside of what I now know to be audacity to ask about my son, whose massive picture was still at my desk from when my coworkers announced my delivery while I was still out on maternity leave.

It was the Tuesday before Thanksgiving (we were off that Wednesday), and six months since Tonia started, when my manager called me into Tonia's office. I thought it was odd that when I got into the office, I only saw my manager—no Tonia. All of a sudden, her patronizing voice came through the speaker of the 1992 desk phone. She began with her phony pleasantries, and then:

"Well, after much thought and deliberation, I have decided that based on your tardiness, I will have to let you go, effective today."

My heart dropped. My manager couldn't even look me in the eyes. She and I had known each other prior to her becoming my new manager, and we had built a rather friendly relationship, but at that moment, she couldn't speak. I worked for the company for almost three years, and I was not only a high performer, but I also got along with everyone and caused no issues. I will admit I had been tardy three times within the six months; however, it was always within five to ten minutes of the start of the shift, and I always called ahead. To be honest, I thought that I was doing pretty well navigating my new schedule with a nine-month-old plus Troy, but none of that mattered now. I was being fired two days before Thanksgiving, and on speakerphone, no less. The more her words simmered, the more disrespected I felt.

She asked me if there was anything that I wanted to say. Most times, in a situation like this, I would toss the phony pleasantries back and walk away. But on this particular day, I just could not.

" . . . Not only am I a top performer in my bay—I was also entrusted with PPI (private personal information) and notable company information. I also made sure that people had what they needed while tending to the high-volume front desk on top of my day-to-day work, without any additional compensation. You may believe that I'm just a number, but you'll find that my level of quality will always outweigh quantity. Might I add that I find it disrespectful that you not only decided to terminate me before the holidays, but you didn't even have the respect enough to do it in person."

To this day, I don't regret one word, and those I know who remained at the company continued to complain in dismay.

On the way home, I was so upset that all I could do was cry. I had been so comfortable in that role that even when I would think about leaving, I would tell myself, *Stay just a little bit longer . . . until the baby gets a little older*, even though I knew I could be making more money elsewhere. As the tears rolled down my face, in my mind, I saw a picture of my son. Here I was, again having this inner realization: *I am an unmarried woman, with a child . . . with NO JOB.* I wouldn't say that God laughed at that moment, but I'm sure He was looking down and saying, "Ye of little faith" (Matt 8:26).

I had never felt as low as I did going home to tell Troy that I had lost my job. It was the first of its kind for me, and I'm sure I would've handled the news differently had this happened a year or so ahead of time, but my entire perspective had changed with having a baby involved. I cried as I shared the news. Troy wanted to console me more than he did, but I knew that the thought of him shouldering all of the weight of the household was quickly settling in.

Four slow months went by. We saved money in daycare costs because I stayed home with Trey. I don't even remember what I did during the days other than applying to jobs and going to interviews. I was miserable. It wasn't until one day in March when I had my daily talk with God that things began to REALLY change for me.

I was sitting in Trey's nursery, and, up until this point, I had been stoic. I cleaned; I cooked; I took care of Trey; I did whatever needed to be done. However, on this day, the truism of having been out of work for four months was more than I could bear. I had been on multiple conference calls with Tonia and the state's unemployment office, as she had been fighting tooth and nail to see to it that I did not receive compensation.

I appealed the case twice, and she showed up for each call. Had she not shown up to just one, I would've won my case. However, she had built up a storyline to make me look like someone who didn't take their job seriously simply because I had been late those three times. It didn't matter that I had called; it didn't matter that I was a new mom; it didn't matter that I lived almost an hour away; it didn't matter that I was within ten minutes of the shift starting; it didn't matter that everyone in that company knew my caliber and standard of work.

I was dealing with a demonic spirit. It was my first time as an adult going to battle on a spiritual front. As the tears welled up, I spoke out loud:

"God, I'm angry . . . I'm sad . . . I'm lost, and I can't see what's ahead. I need You to take control of my situation. Show me what it is that I'm supposed to learn, and allow me to move forward. I need You to show up and show out for Your child. Renew my heart, renew my mind, and renew the right spirit within me (Psalms 51:10)."

And just like that, I had hope again.

Having worked in Washington, D.C., as a professional recruiter for such companies as the World Bank, the Motley Fool, and Rolls-Royce, I knew what to put on my résumé, and I knew what employers wanted to hear. Yet, it was as if I was being blocked from landing the positions that I was going after. Because Virginia is more of a service area, you aren't going to find many large businesses headquartered here, which narrowed my search.

After competing for three positions, getting to the last round in each, and getting beaten by the competition, that flicker of hope was beginning to dim again. One day, my mother asked me, "Have you thought about getting a recruiter yourself?" I thought for a moment, *Perhaps I thought I knew it all—I had been a recruiter myself, after all*, but really, the thought hadn't even crossed my mind to put one to work on my behalf. I took her advice, and I was called for an open requisition within two days.

Upon my arrival, my recruiter begged me to work for their firm instead of interviewing for the open requisition. I told him recruiting was no longer for me and that I was looking forward to something new. Depending on the position, recruiters don't always divulge the name of the company that you'll interview with. That was the case here. I arrived on the third floor of a tall executive tower; the name of the company occupying the suite was nondescript. I was greeted by a woman who I could tell was already in her third trimester of pregnancy.

"Jasmine?" she asked.

"Yes!" I anxiously replied.

"I'm Nicole. It's so nice to meet you. Please follow me," she insisted.

When we arrived at the interview room, waiting there was a young lady who assisted Nicole with questions. The interview felt more like a blind date than the average probe and pressure to explain why I was better than everyone else they had interviewed. I felt like they wanted to ensure that the person who would assume this role completely fit the job culture was proficient in their skills, yet coachable and open to new ways of thinking. After answering the last question, Nicole closed by saying:

"I'll be leaving for maternity leave in a month, and I want to ensure that the person we hire can learn the role quickly and execute at a high level. After speaking with you today, I believe we've found who we've been looking for, and if it's okay with you, we'd like you to be the last person we interview. If you decide to accept, you'll be reporting to NASA beginning in two weeks."

I was in complete shock. Not only did I not know that there was a NASA center where I lived, but the mere thought of God's favor to give me this opportunity just seemed unreal. I was completely in awe of God's grace and mercy. All of those times when I couldn't understand what was happening and I didn't know why things weren't happening in the way I wanted them to, God was working in the background all along to give me hope and a future (Jeremiah 29:11). He exceeded my expectations, and again, He laughed.

I humbly accepted my new role, and I assumed my position the Monday after that Mother's Day. In the years to follow, God would continue to show up and show out in my life. My life has not been perfect, but it has been God-ordained; I have been favored throughout, and I'll take that over perfection every single time.

Jasmine Byrd and Troy Whiting, Jr. married on May 28, 2022.

Jasmine Byrd-Whiting

Chapter 7

BRUISED BUT BLESSED

This is dedicated to my parents for teaching me how to pray, to my son for strengthening me at my weakest, to my love for choosing me, to my sugar babies for the joy you bring me, to my friend who never judged me and was always there for me, and to all the prayer warriors who prayed for and with me.

It was Easter weekend 1970 in Central Park Projects, and most of the parents in our neighborhood in the projects were getting their kids ready for Easter Sunday. The meals were being prepared; you could smell the collard greens, hog maws and chitterlings, ham, fried chicken, green beans, macaroni and cheese, potatoes being prepared for potato salad, yams baking in the oven, banana pudding, sweet potato pie, and cornbread. Oh, yeah—my siblings and I would have Kool-Aid and lemonade to wash it all down, and our parents would have soda. Mama and Daddy had purchased our fancy Easter Sunday's best outfits: one for Easter Sunday morning, one for after church so we could hunt for eggs and enjoy ourselves, and the last one for Easter Sunday evening to say our speeches. We'd been practicing our speeches for weeks. We got our hair done on Saturday.

"Mama, I want my hair straightened just like hers; she's so pretty," I pleaded. "She's my big sister and my first best friend."

Well, the answer again this year was still no. It would be five years later, when I was ten years old, that I had the experience of the infamous hot comb or Marcel curling iron touching my hair. After our hair was done and we got ready for bed, a stocking cap and scarf would be placed on our heads so tightly that in the morning, our hair would look like it was just done, and we wouldn't be late to church for Sunday school.

When my eldest sister, who was four years my senior and five grades ahead of me, became pregnant at the young age of thirteen, my parents almost lost their minds and quickly went into lockdown mode. They were determined I would not be next, although I was only in the fifth grade. Their determination was in full effect. Things did change for our family. I remember finishing fifth grade full of excitement, running home, shouting, "It's summertime!" I got off the school bus and headed to our apartment in the projects. There was a moving van, and our house was almost empty.

My reaction was to exclaim, in my loud and outspoken voice, "What in the world are y'all doing?"

Did I mention that I was a very loud and outspoken kid? I asked what was going on and was told, "We're moving. Grab a box." *Moving? They have lost their minds!* I thought. This was God's favor over my life, but I was too young to see it or understand it. Needless to say, my siblings and I were all distraught and in disbelief. The way we were crying and carrying on, you would have thought somebody had died. I said to my parents, "This is where all of my friends live." Even the ones I had to fight regularly were still my friends.

My sister is, and always has been, so beautiful and easygoing. She was not a fighter or loud, so I would fight for her if and when I had to. She didn't want to move, either. Well, once we came to our senses, it goes without saying that we fell in love with our new neighborhood and very large home. God's favor was all over us, and we were too young to know it then. We all made new friends and still kept in touch with our friends in the projects, too!

My sister gave birth to her first child the same summer we moved, at the tender age of fourteen. We all welcomed a beautiful baby girl. I loved her so much, but I didn't like that she had taken my first best friend from me. The following year, my sister had another beautiful daughter, and eight months later, my mom gave birth to baby number ten: my beautiful baby sister. As the seventh child, I thought, *They are just having too many babies.* I told my mom, "Now, everybody is going to be saying, 'Her Mama has ten children.' I can't even believe you still having babies!" I was so outspoken at times and always loud. My Mama used to say, "Girls are supposed to be seen and not heard." Needless to say, I fell in love with number ten.

I took my baby sister as my very own—at least, in my head and my heart—since my role model had two, and my parents had others to care for. So, she was perfect for me. My big sister finished high school and left for college, and I became the full-time assistant caregiver to her two girls, along with my three younger siblings. My parents were overprotective of me and wanted to make sure that I, too, would not become a teen mother. Those times were tough, and, sometimes, I felt like I was paying for a debt I didn't owe. God's favor protected me through the guidance of my parents.

When I was in junior high school, I met someone who would become my best friend. After hanging out and sharing our thoughts and feelings, we decided that we would like to become cheerleaders. So, we tried out for the team and made it. We talked almost every day, and the summer of 1979 right before our sophomore year, we applied to the only local vocational-technical high school. Six weeks later, I received an acceptance letter and called my best friend to see if she had received an acceptance letter. We were both so excited to know that we were about to start high school.

"What's your bus number, and what stop will you be getting on?"

"Girl, can you believe it? We are going to be attending Tech!"

"Girl, we are almost grown!"

My best friend and I talked about everything, including our boyfriends who had enlisted in the military and would be leaving soon. We talked about what we wanted to be when we finished school, when we could leave our parents' homes and be out on our own, what type of house and cars we were going to buy for ourselves, and owning our own hair salon.

Three weeks into high school, I was telling my best friend that my boyfriend was leaving:

"Yes, girl, you know he is leaving for basic training in a couple of weeks. I can't believe he joined the military. All I know is he'd better come back and marry me and take me around the world with him."

I loved him with all my heart and soul, so I was going to wait for him to come back for me. I was young—fourteen—but my mind was made-up: *I will be his wife one day.*

My sister was attending a private HBCU in Florida, near the beach. While in high school, I was blessed to visit her for my spring breaks. I was so proud of her for not dropping out of school because she became a teen mom, and I was also jealous of her for being away at college. My big sis's college life looked fabulous, full of happy times and pledging. I started planning in my head: *In a few years, I, too, am going to college.* I wanted to go to the big city of Atlanta and attend the all-girls college, but my dad said that life was too fast for me. I guess my dad must have known my intentions. Dad knew what was best for me because he worked in Atlanta for a while, and as sure as the day was long, I was going to Atlanta to party, party, and party some more. It was the biggest city I had ever seen.

My high school years went by fast and oh-so-slow, too. It seemed like only yesterday that my best friend and I were cheerleaders, and now, we were almost adults at the age of seventeen. Eighteen was the legal age, but the legal age for consuming alcohol changed to twenty-one the year we graduated from high school. We attended the vocational-technical high school of our dreams, and our trade was cosmetology. I was great at my trade; I competed in several competitions with some losses and some amazing wins. I won first place in my region and second place in the state.

Time waits for no one. *I am a senior in high school, and soon, I will be on my own at college somewhere. All I know is, I am going to party every night.* Hmmm—so I thought.

Well, life changes, and love will change things, too. Let me tell you, I was now an engaged high school senior . . . *Yessss!* I called my best friend to tell her my news. We were out of school for Christmas break.

"Girl, guess what? You ain't gonna believe this!" I was filled with so much love, joy, and excitement. "He asked me to marry him, and I said yes! Hell, yeah!"

I had waited for three years for this magic man to return home to me from the military as I remained a virgin until a few months before our wedding. I prayed hard, asking for God's forgiveness because I knew better than to have sex outside of marriage. Thankfully, one of my childhood friends, who had become a teen mom, encouraged me to get on birth control pills months earlier.

Although I was a virgin, her sincerest and most honest words to me were, "It is better to have birth control pills and not need them than to need them and not have them." And, with that statement, I got up the nerve and went to my mom to get her to sign the permission document and the five dollars it would cost to see the doctor at our local health department. The physical for the birth control pills did a number on me and my virgin vagina, so much so that the nurse who conducted the physical asked me what I was doing there. I replied with the statement my friend told me: "It's better to have birth control pills and not need them than to need them and not have them."

She replied, "You have a very wise and caring friend."

Once again, God's favor was on my life, protecting me and covering me from myself. I met my fiance when I was fourteen and in the ninth grade. He was kind and handsome. He was a senior in high school in another school district when we met and started courting. Yes, I said courting—it's when a guy comes to visit you and your family.

The two of us were never alone, and the visits were not only short, but they were also awkward. Parents always ask, "Who are your folks? Where are they from? Where do you live?" My parents were serious, and this was how they communicated with the young man to see if he came from a good family and what his intentions for courting their daughter were.

With the girls on my heels, you can rest assured there was no hanky panky or they would have spilled their little guts and I wouldn't be alive to tell the story. My baby sister and my two nieces were ages one, two, and three. The three toddlers were the youngest of the five children in the house, and I was now the big sister, Auntie, and second-in-command to my mom. I cooked meals and cleaned like a woman twenty years my senior. My mom kept a very clean home, so we learned from the best. She taught me how to prepare full meals by the age of eleven—and I'd better not burn the food because that was lazy and wasteful. The youngest three girls consisted of my sister's two girls and my youngest baby sister; those three were with me at all times. If I had to go to the corner store, they were with me; when I went down the street to visit my friend, they were with me. Those three were my first birth control—okay, maybe my first birth control was fear because my parents did not play.

Our move from the projects brought about change; Dad became a preacher when we moved from the projects, and all the family cookouts were now being held at our huge home located on a massive corner lot. Dad got a second job, and Mom maintained her job as a cook with the Board of Education. Mom was also the enforcer and regulator at home. At times, Mom would sound like a sailor to get all of us kids in line, mainly me and one of my older brothers because the other kids knew better and weren't as hardheaded. Sometimes, she would say, "Don't play with me. I don't play with children. I don't even play the radio," through tight lips, with a serious stare. That statement was the absolute truth, and she meant it. I have never seen my mom turn on the radio, but she allowed us to, especially on Saturdays when we were cleaning and on Sunday mornings to listen to gospel music or catch the radio preacher selling prayer cloths. However, that was us, not my mom. My mom was a loving and level-headed woman. My mom used to always say, "I want you all to be better than me. Get your high school diploma and go to college; don't depend on no one else."

Dad was hardworking and exposed us to many wonderful things, like going to Disney World in Orlando, Florida regularly or walking downtown to get fresh fruit and ice cream cones. One of the best family experiences was the trip to Atlanta, Georgia. We stayed in a fancy hotel with a shopping mall and were treated to a mini shopping spree. They were blessed with hardworking, wonderful, and loving parents. The most valuable tool they blessed us with was knowing God and how to pray. We had our share of life situations and circumstances, but through our relationship with God, we overcame tough times.

He Purchased the Ring

In early January 1983 of my senior year, my boyfriend picked me up after school to take me ring shopping. We found a ring that we both liked and that he could afford. He put the ring on my hand. I told my parents that I was getting married, and they were not having that. My mom said I was too young; I didn't know anything about being married. My dad said he didn't have any girls to give away, and that was that. Well, one of my eldest brothers got my mom's attention and suggested they support me—I was going to do it with or without them.

My mom then convinced my dad to consent to my marriage. I promised that if they let me get married, I would go to college and make them proud. My dad agreed to perform the ceremony, and my big brother gave me away. Funny thing: Both of my parents had to sign for me to get married because I was only seventeen. I finished high school that June and was married exactly thirty days later in July. The ceremony was absolutely beautiful.

My mom's friends catered the food, and my dress was borrowed from my sister-in-law who married my brother the previous December. My godmother purchased my flowers, and my favorite school counselor did the music for the ceremony. I had saved up enough money to help my parents rent the hall where the reception was being held. My fourteen-layer cake for one hundred and fifty dollars was a bargain from a baker who was just starting their cake business. God's favor and goodness have always covered me.

My husband was my first love, and I trusted him with everything—especially my heart! Now, I was growing up faster than I thought or imagined. You know, by now, I was real grown, married at seventeen, and I knew everything. I knew how to pray, read God's word, and seek His blessing in our lives.

We had a good honeymoon. One of the gifts we received from a friend was a book of food stamps (yes, they used to come in a booklet). With those food stamps, we purchased cold cuts, condiments, bread, and chips. We made sandwiches for the next couple of days, and we had enough money for Slurpees, my favorite drink. My loving and handsome husband had to return to his duty station and would send for me when he secured a place for us to stay. I could hardly wait to be with him, no matter where we would live. I received a call in mid-August that we had a beautiful two-story apartment. A week later, I was on the commercial bus for my twelve-hour ride, heading to a place I had never seen, located three states over from where I grew up.

Today, as I look back over my life and think about how my parents did not want me to be a teen mother, I thank God for those overprotective parents. Funny how the tables turn; I think I am just like them in many ways. I find myself feeling like they must have felt because today, I am raising one of my son's daughters. She has been with us since 2007, when she was one going on two, and now, she is this strikingly beautiful seventeen-year-old with a very active young life; this is her senior year in high school. She is an author, a competitive cheerleader, and a school cheerleader.

She is my heart, along with her younger sister who, too, is an author at the young age of ten. She currently resides in another state. The seventeen-year-old big sister is at the age of dating, and things are so different from when her dad was a teenager and most definitely different from when I was her age. She sometimes reminds me of myself in the sense she can't wait to be grown. I pray over my family, and I trust that she, too, will remember what I have taught her: to always pray and ask for wisdom.

Prayer and faith were powerful tools my parents must have used when they allowed me to marry and move away at seventeen to live like an experienced grown woman at such a young age.

On the bus ride to see my husband, my magic man, there were no cell phones, only phone booths along the way to make collect calls letting him know my status and whereabouts. I arrived at my destination wearing my favorite black pants and my favorite red and black top. Nervous as all get-out, I was so excited to be on my own that my menstrual cycle started, and my husband had to go out and purchase me some sanitary products . . . *Ha!* I had very little experience in the bedroom, so my cycle gave me more time to get my nerves in order.

September is my birthday month and is usually one of the happiest months of the year for me—and now it was for him, too! We both were born in September. Well, this particular September was not so happy; truth be told, it was one of the most terrifying and hurtful times of my young, newlywed life! We had to go to the military clinic to be tested for possibly being exposed to or having a sexually transmitted disease (STD). This is when I had to use what I had been taught. I had to pray and cry out to God Almighty for help in a way that I had never done or needed to do before. *God, HELP ME! I took a vow for better or worse. If I leave now, I will be a failure, and I am too strong for that*—not to mention, I loved him no matter what, and I didn't want to go back to that strict home. *God, help me. Show me what to do.*

The test results were negative—thank God. So, I prayed, and I stayed, but I had a million questions and was very scared. Although the results were "negative" and I was still learning how to please my husband in bed, I became very apprehensive when it came time to have sex. As I matured in life, much later in life, it went from

176

having sex to making love, and there is a difference. However, in time, I eventually got past the scare. I put my best foot forward and my best look on so no one could ever see my pain.

I functioned comfortably in my new situation, and just when I thought I was mentally getting better from one disappointment, here came another one: My husband's ex-girlfriend had gotten pregnant, and she said the baby was his. How could this be if we were faithful to each other and we'd just gotten married? Well, he confessed that he had sex with her the night before we got married.

Although I appreciated his honesty, it really took my breath away and knocked me down in private, but I refused to let anyone see me hurting or think they had a one-up on me. Believe me, the waiting was brutal at times, but I know prayer changes things. We would go home on leave for holidays and special occasions, and she would always make her way over to his mom's home. I felt like she was taunting me, but I was not being moved. I held my head high and stood amid great hurt and disappointment, and I was not going to let anyone discredit this perfect marriage or the perfect man. I know there was good in him, and he was young, so I stayed with him. He asked for forgiveness and gave me his word that he would never hurt or disappoint me again.

After holding my breath for almost a year, the DNA test revealed that her newborn son was not my husband's. Thank You, God, for Your favor and for the strength to stand during that storm. While waiting for the results of that test, we planned to conceive a child of our own. This was the happiest time of my life—until it wasn't. I was very sick during my pregnancy, but I kept my head up and my appearance stellar, prepared meals daily, and kept a very spotless home.

During my pregnancy, I volunteered at the Army Community Center to gain some work experience because I didn't have any at the time. As time went on, the pregnancy became more difficult, and my parents suggested that I come to their home so that they could take care of me. My husband agreed, so for the last three months of my pregnancy, I was in my home state with my parents and other family members caring for me. It was a blessing. You see, my best friend had gotten married and was also expecting her first child; sometimes, we both had our doctor appointments together.

In February 1985, our sons were born two weeks apart. Unfortunately, my husband was unable to witness the birth of our son, but he came as soon as he could. In the meantime, my mom and big sister were there to support and pray for me. I think they knew I was sad that he couldn't be there for me, and I felt alone. My husband stayed with us for the first week, and then he had to return to work. Our son and I stayed with my parents for six more weeks before returning to our home.

When our son and I returned from my parents' home, I thought that my husband would be excited and overjoyed to see me after having been gone so long. Well, after being back in our home for about a month, something just didn't seem right . . . and, unfortunately, my intuition was right. I found out that while I was away, my husband was involved in another relationship, and that person became pregnant. He moved out of our home and moved in with his mistress. As you can imagine, I felt hurt, disappointed, and betrayed again—only this time, my strength was failing. I had had enough.

I called my parents to tell them I wasn't happy, and they prayed for and with me, but I just couldn't handle much more. I never told anyone what was going on, only that I wasn't happy and that I didn't think he loved me. My dad was angry about how his daughter had been treated, but he refused to come and get me. His exact words were, "If I go and get her, she can never go back." As I was dealing with this trauma, I began to regain my strength and muster up some self-pride. I made one of the toughest and smartest decisions in my young life, and that was to leave my husband and go back to my parents' home. They sent three of my siblings to come get me and my son.

The mistress said that she had a miscarriage.

As I walked out the door of my military post home, I promised my husband that I wouldn't look back, and I didn't. I held my head up high and walked past him to get into the car with my siblings. The ride home was long, and it gave me some time to think about my marriage, my future, and our son's future. I began to think about what I wanted, so I enrolled in medical assistant school. By this time, my son was about six months old. When I completed school, he was a little older than one year old. With my husband being persistent with his visits and begging for his family, I ultimately returned to our post and started my externship at a women's clinic.

I thought things were going well and that we were going to be the family I desired and deserved—but not so fast! Here comes *another* blow! Too embarrassing to give all the details, but I will say I almost caved in and wanted to give up on life. I was so distraught and in disbelief. *This can't be how life is. Maybe I am not pretty enough.* I didn't feel that I was shapely enough, mainly because he looked at other women in my presence, sometimes as if I wasn't there. I thought everything was wrong with me. I thought maybe it was my chipped tooth or my lack of experience in the bedroom.

Or is it the last two statements he said to me: "Babies don't make a marriage" and "I do love her"?

I could not believe that the man I married, who I loved with every fiber of my being and shared a beautiful son with, just uttered those words to me! I sank to the floor and began weeping and wailing. At some point, I grabbed a bottle of pills and contemplated suicide. I know God kept me! Right at the moment I got the bottle open, my precious baby woke up, lifted his beautiful head, and smiled at me. Whew! I tell you, that very moment changed my life.

I prayed, got up off the floor, and promised myself that I would never give up on life and will not leave my baby here for someone else to care for him. My son was planned, I chose him, and I was determined to give him my absolute best, even if I had to suffer through broken promises, disappointments, and heartbreaks. I would be strong for him.

We were blessed with orders and moved to Europe. We traveled the world, we had some great times, and I learned to function in the not-so-great times. I let the world see a pretty darn perfect marriage and a beautiful family. At times, there was no pretending;

when we came together as one, we were unstoppable, and I felt some love. I refused to let anyone see my pain. I promised myself that I would not have the family of five that I so desired, and with that, I only had one child.

As we traveled around the world from one military installation to the next, it was challenging to gain higher education. I applied for a job at the military hospital and was told I didn't qualify. Thank God for the many amazing friends and adopted parents/families I met on my journey as a military spouse. I ran into a good friend while leaving the commissary. The commissary is the military grocery store, located on the installation. This friend did not know—and neither did I—that she was really about to change my life with her words of wisdom and encouragement.

At this time, I had been out of high school for almost ten years, and my hope and desire to attend college were looking bleak. She provided clear guidance on how to get started and be successful. Let me say, I was scared; I had such a fear of going to college at that point. *It's ten years after high school, and we are at a new duty station,* I thought—that in itself could be fearful and challenging. I had a marriage and a young child to care for, and I was unemployed. I faced my paralyzing fear with mustard seed faith, prayer, and continuous encouragement from my friends and family.

The first two courses went better than I had expected. God's phenomenal favor and that unemployment check were a great help in supporting those first two courses. Things were going pretty well until I received notice that my unemployment was ending. I had been looking everywhere for a job, and nothing was coming through for me. Although I was married, I still believed in being a help to my husband and our household. Whew! Let me tell you, God is truly an on-time God! This particular Wednesday morning, I had taken my handsome second-grader to school, dropped him off, and gone home to do some cleaning and prepare dinner when reality hit me hard. I walked into our apartment knowing I had received my last unemployment check, which helped out with groceries, gas, and my college courses. I remember trying to be strong, so I started praying. Then, the fear brought on tears, but mustard seed faith began to move mountains. I started singing, "I don't believe He brought me this far to leave me."

I was still crying, singing, and praying when the phone rang. I answered it; there was no caller ID. I was trying to sound as normal as possible so the person on the other end couldn't tell I was crying. The kind and soft voice on the other end introduced herself to me and presented one of my most memorable breakthroughs. She offered me a temporary job with the federal government as a telephone operator at the nearby Air Force base, and a couple of months later, my position became permanent. Again, I had just received God's favor. I chose to work the hours most people didn't want, and that's the third shift: 11:00 p.m. to 7:00 a.m. I worked that shift with an angel on Earth. She was an older woman with the same name as my mother, and she knew my situation. Every night we worked together, she would bring my lunch and send me into the connecting room to study. God is so amazing.

This job allowed me to help my husband, helped support my education, and gave me quality time with my son. Some of the time with my son may not have always been fun. I started working a part-time job at his school and started attending college at night, so there were times when he had to go to class with me and sit in the back, playing on his Game Boy quietly. I had planned on just two classes at a time until the military started making changes that affected us and threatened my husband's military career. He began attending college with me. I began taking a full load before we would have to relocate.

His support helped me because we were able to take several courses together, and he motivated me through some of my toughest courses. With the possibility of him not being able to retire hanging in the balance, I began looking into programs that would put me on a fast track to promotion within the federal government. The stress was on because I wanted my family to continue to live a fairly decent life. The programs required a bachelor's degree and finishing with a three-point-five grade point average. We both finished our associate's degrees, and we graduated together. By God's grace and favor, he was allowed to reenlist for the last time; this reenlistment would take him into his twenty years, and he would be eligible for retirement. Shortly after completing our associate's degrees, we were transferred to our last duty station together.

When we arrived there, we did not have housing yet, and two of our very dear friends opened their homes to us. We stayed a month with one, and then my son and I went to stay with my big brother, who was also in the military and stationed at the base in the next state over from us. Our time there was very memorable and meaningful to my family.

I recall attending church service at a local church, and a woman minister was speaking and teaching that Sunday. Her message was so profound that I still use her teachings today: "Write down what you want God to do for you." Well, I took that message to heart, and I began writing down everything I wanted to be blessed with. One of the things I wanted for my family and myself was to obtain a bachelor's degree. I talked with my family—mainly my son, who was now in the fifth grade. I talked with my big brother and my sister-in-law, asking if they would watch my son and support me as I went to the HBCU near our base, but just until we got housing.

We decided to stay with one of our friends while I attended the local HBCU to work toward obtaining my bachelor's degree so I could get accepted into the federal government's fast-track training program. Once again, I was starting with an unemployment check and mustard seed faith. My dear friend not only allowed us to live with her until our housing was available, but she gave us her room, and she slept on a mattress in her living room. Not one time did she ever make us feel uncomfortable or unwanted.

We received housing a few months later, and I was offered a job at the military hospital. I was able to bring my son home with us. I had a full load in college and worked a full-time job.

I gave my best effort to fulfill my promise to myself and my parents. I finished college with honors. The young girl who got married and left home at seventeen with dreams of going to college and partying can now look at her parents proudly—and, on Mother's Day weekend in 1998, I walked across the stage to receive my bachelor's degree with honors, magna cum laude. A few years later, my parents and family witnessed me receiving my master's degree. My desire and promise of attending college were fulfilled.

I also wrote down *BUY A NEW HOME* and put a price on it that I thought we could afford. I made my list and put it away for about seven years straight, and I tell you, God not only honored my prayer request—I was blessed exceedingly and abundantly, above what I could have ever requested. My heart still says, "Thank You, Lord!" I know God's phenomenal favor is still all over my life. We survived over thirty years of marriage. As I reflect and look back over my life and all that God has brought me through, I am eternally grateful. My soul says, "Yes, Lord!" I am a witness that God's favor is phenomenal, and it is real for me. I am older and wiser, and I know what love is.

Peaches Blu

Chapter 8

COUNT IT ALL JOY

To my family, those here with me and those in heaven. Thank you for your prayers, your love, and your guidance. You taught us well, and we continue to be recipients of the things you went to God for on our behalf. To my parents, George and Roxanne, thank you for your presence. You have created the blueprint, and my children are loving, confident, and wise beyond their years. Thank you, Mama, for your words and your love for Papa. Your example of everlasting love has taught me so much. Thank you, Quavon, for loving all of me and granting me the greatest gifts in this world: Eden and Quinn. My love for you has no bounds; my prayer is that you grow, always knowing how much you are valued and loved.

Part I

"I was a good girl, always listened to Mama, but I loved your grandfather, and the only time I disobeyed her was when I got pregnant."

I remembered my grandmother drilling those words into me as a teenager, and after hearing from the nurse in McVicker, those words permeated through me in a way they had never before. My grandmother, "Mama" as I, the first grandchild, named her, had my mother at only sixteen years old. She married the love of her life, my grandfather, a few years later, but the stain that being an unwed, teenage mother in the 1950s left on our family was one that still impacts us in one way or another to this very day.

Like Mama, I listened to my mother. Being a good daughter was among the things I was most proud of and also what I worked hardest to maintain. Being a good daughter also meant that I was a good student, a good Christian young lady, and, without a doubt, would become a good wife, mother, and likely a good lawyer because that's what I had been saying since at least the age of eleven. My grandmother didn't get to attend college, so my mom became a first-generation college student.

Mama had Mommy out of wedlock, so my mom got married right out of college and didn't have me until seven years later. That cycle had ended, but here I was a month into my freshman year at Spelman—in the infirmary because, after weeks of headaches and cramps with no period, the diagnosis was simple: a positive pregnancy test. I sat on that news for days. Sat, slept, stayed up all night.

How was I going to explain this? Forget explaining—how was I even going to tell my mother? The same mother who had cried tears of joy just a few weeks ago. We shared such a heartfelt goodbye and didn't plan on reuniting until Thanksgiving. I would

190

assume news like this should be delivered or at least dealt with in person, but HOW would I even approach such a thing? Especially when midterms were just a few weeks away, and I had finally found my rhythm living on campus. I knew that time was ticking and that this wasn't something that I could keep to myself for too long.

I didn't go a day without speaking to my mom, so it became harder and harder to have regular conversations without saying what needed to be said. So, one evening, after catching up on *General Hospital* like we normally did, talking about what was new with Sonny and Carly . . .

I said, "So, I finally went to the doctor. I know why I've been having those cramps . . . "

I remember my voice fading. I hadn't had the nerve to actually say "it" aloud, and even at that moment, I was pretty sure I wouldn't be able to make those words come out. There was silence.

"Well? What did they say?" my mom asked. Then, almost immediately, she followed with, "You're pregnant, aren't you?"

My instant sobs confirmed the answer. "How did you know?"

How DID she know? I didn't even know, and I know that at eighteen and in college, nobody had to notify her.

"I'm your mother. I felt it. I was just waiting for you to tell me so we could figure this all out."

And we figured it out. I don't remember when the decision was made; I don't really recall a conversation in which we decided what the outcome would be. I just remember making some calls, booking a flight home, and showing up for the necessary appointments. Much of the details remain a blur, bits and pieces of the process.

My mom, my biggest supporter and confidant, was the only person to know, and of the things I do remember, the thing that sticks out most is walking through the protesters and one directing their anger to her: "THAT IS YOUR GRANDCHILD! HOW COULD YOU?" I remember her palm on the small of my back—always there, always protecting me, always reminding me to walk straight and keep my head up high.

I don't remember much of the process. Honestly, what I remember most is making sure I got a doctor's note to exempt me from my Water Aerobics class (my physical education credit) and then making it back to campus late Sunday evening so I wouldn't miss my 8 a.m. Monday class. There was no significant healing to speak of—not physically or mentally. Once I made it back to Atlanta, it was pretty much business as usual.

I never mentioned it to my new college friends. In fact, I never even talked about it with my friends from home. I didn't discuss it, I didn't think about it; I kind of just bounced back and moved along. I did mentally calculate what may have been my due date, and when that time came, I would think about how different things would have been.

I came to terms with the choice that was made, I came to terms with the decision, and I don't remember exactly when, but guilt crept in. I felt guilty and ashamed, and because it was easier not to talk about it, I just kept those feelings to myself. Those feelings—

sometimes big, sometimes small—became a hidden part of me. They showed up in lots of different ways, in lots of decisions that I made. I started to believe that this one decision, this one choice, changed my life, and that if good things didn't happen, it was my punishment.

Part II

"Feelings aren't facts, kiddo. They're just feelings. What are you going to do with them?"

My dad is a social worker, and oftentimes, I would go to him, hoping for some comforting advice. Instead, he would "social work" me, and while I didn't often feel good about his responses, I learned how to take things as they were and not just how I perceived them to be.

So, in the years between my freshman year and college graduation, I learned to balance how I felt about myself and different situations—whether good or bad—and what was actually happening. But that also pushed me into a very concrete way of thinking; I lived in a black-and-white world. I saw things as either completely right or completely wrong, all or nothing. No room for nuance; no shades of gray. The choices I made, the choices those around me made—they all came with either a reward or a consequence.

When I was about twenty-one, after a referral from my OB-GYN, I went to a specialist who conducted several tests, an ultrasound, and bloodwork. I'll never forget how the doctor prefaced what he was about to tell me:

"I am surprised that you were able to get pregnant. You were young, so that may explain it, BUT I imagine when and if you want to conceive, it'll be a challenge." He continued, "I don't like to speak in absolutes, but with PCOS and what I'm seeing from your tests, it'll certainly be an uphill battle."

I don't remember having much of a reaction. Hearing those words felt like confirmation of what I'd already assumed: I made a choice that would change the trajectory of my life, and my only chances of being a mother were over. I told my mom, and she, always being the voice of reason, said, "At twenty-one, this isn't even something you should be worrying about. When the time is right, you will be just fine." I accepted her answer, but I still felt guilty—and again, because it was easier not to talk about it, I just kept those feelings to myself.

During this time, I continued to do what I always did . . . what I was supposed to do: I graduated, jumped right into my career, and then started graduate school. I worked hard, and I partied hard, too. I'm not sure if it was self-sabotage or insecurity, or if I just needed a break from doing everything as I was expected to. I drank more than I should've, partied more than I should've, and found myself in countless situations that I realize I got out of only because of God's grace protecting me.

I've been in church my whole life, and throughout a lot of my life, church was routine. It was the Sunday morning thing to do. So, no matter what I did Saturday night, I got up, got dressed, and made my way to church. I got complacent in that routine, but looking

194

back, it was that foundation that kept me through the worst of my choices—both the good and bad.

Looking back further, that was favor—God's favor. Despite what I did, God was still there for me. Protecting me, keeping me, blessing me . . . in spite of me.

I was single, and when I wasn't, who I was with wasn't who I was meant to be with. Although I forced situationships, I knew I deserved better, and if I never got any better, then that was a consequence. Everyone in my life was disposable—friends, potential partners, even family. I thought I was creating boundaries when I was really creating walls. I withheld from others the grace that God had and would continue to give me.

Part III

I often wonder if other people remember the exact moment they decided to change—if they remember what prompted the shift in their life and not only what caused it but the details of the minute that would likely change the direction of their life. For me, that moment was in front of a Popeyes at about 2:30 a.m. after a night of drinking at the bar. Once again, my friends and I had been followed from the club. Somebody's mad baby momma or ex-girlfriend or current girlfriend or whatever variation wanted to yell, scream, and fight in the parking lot that night.

I was tired. I knew this was ridiculous. I was over it, and even after two friends hopped out to yell, scream, and fight back . . . I just sat in the car. I couldn't do it. I didn't care whose man it was about this time. I was over the same thing weekend after weekend.

I wasn't necessarily looking for an escape, but God still provided a ram in the bush.

Out of nowhere, a friend who had no reason to be at Popeyes at 2 a.m. appeared at the door.

He said, "Come on. You don't need to be here. Get in the car with me. You should go home."

And that is exactly what I did.

Normally, I wouldn't dare leave my friends. Normally, I would hop right amid all the chaos, all the confusion, all the drama. But that night, I went home. I turned my ringer off and went to sleep. I didn't worry about what happened. I didn't wonder if the yelling turned into actual fighting. I took a shower and slept like a baby.

I remember waking up the next morning. My alarm was set at 6:30 a.m. every Sunday morning so I could make 7:30 service. I would aim for 7:30 service so that I would be out and home by 9:30 . . . I would nap and still have plenty of time for brunch. If 7:30 a.m. service didn't happen, I would go to 9:30 service, which would have me home by 11:30, still with plenty of time to enjoy my day. That was my usual routine, but waking up that morning, things felt different.

When I saw all the missed calls and unread text messages, I didn't care to know what happened after I left. It was always the same scenario, anyway. I remember driving to church with a clarity of mind I hadn't felt in a while, if ever before. I'm sure I eventually read the messages and got updated on what happened that night, but I never quite felt the same.

I won't pretend like at that moment, everything stopped. I didn't quit drinking or going out cold turkey, but I did begin to feel more and more out of place when I did decide to go out. I would always drive my own car so I could leave when I wanted. I noticed a change in myself before some of my friends did. I also began to realize who my friends really were and who just enjoyed that side of me.

During this time, how I felt about myself began to change. I started a mental list of pros and cons and realized the pros outweighed the cons. I made some bad choices, and there were things I wasn't proud of—but why, even with those things, was I still a child of the Most High? I was deserving of the blessings that God never withheld from me, even when I didn't believe any good should come to me.

I also began to realize that some of the company I kept had to change. I realized that some of my friends were golden. They loved me for me, and even if I stopped showing up for birthday celebrations at certain clubs, the dynamics of our friendship didn't change.

The dating game also changed. I started to be proud of who I was and more and more optimistic about the lifestyle I wanted and believed God had set out for me. I started to think about who I wanted beside me and realized I needed and wanted someone who I could be proud of; someone who had the same interests, the same type of ambition, and the same love for their family; and someone who knew and had a relationship with Christ.

I remember plainly saying to someone I had been dating, "I'm sorry, but this won't work. I may like you now, but I don't want to wake up in five, ten, or fifteen years and resent you because I had to work extra hard to have the life I want and be embarrassed to introduce you at the job Christmas party." I know that was probably harsh and very hard for him to accept, but I think that realization freed me from a lot of future heartache. I knew very clearly what I wanted, and I was beginning to believe that God was going to give me the desires of my heart.

I started to pay more attention in church. I was serious about really getting to know this Savior that my mom, grandma, and great-grandma depended on. I started taking notes on the sermon and everything. Today, I still look back on those notes I took. The Word began to shape my life, my thinking, my interactions. Looking in the Notes app on my iPhone, on April 5, 2012, I found a declaration and even a ten-year goal:

Instead of doubt, just say, "God, You said," and wait till that becomes, "God, You did!" Take a "You said" approach—"Father, You said I will lend and not borrow." Remind Him of the "You said"s, and don't complain. Remind Him of His promises.

The seed of the righteous is blessed.

As for me and my house, we will serve the Lord.

Father, YOU SAID You would give me beauty for ashes. God, YOU SAID You would pay me back double for the unfair things that have happened. YOU SAID my end will be better than my beginning. YOU SAID the moment I pray, the tide of the battle turns. God, YOU SAID I am more than a conqueror. Many are the afflictions of the righteous, but God, You deliver me from them all.

Present your case based solely on the Word. What He says, He will do.

Ten years from now—the job, family, and children you want. No lack. The Lord will provide.

"Beauty for ashes." "Double." "My end will be better than my beginning." Every morning and all throughout each day, I began to declare God's promises. When things were good, "Beauty. Thank You, Lord." When things were bad, "You will pay me back double; my end will be better. Thank You in advance."

This may seem like where the story shifts, where the fairytale ending starts to play out. I began to change, so, of course, my days would be filled with happiness and blessing after blessing, right? Not exactly. While God is certainly capable of turning around even the worst situation, the most important shift that happened was not in my circumstances but in my perspective.

I began to realize that my mental and emotional well-being literally depended on believing the promises of God. A positive perspective helped me to cultivate a healthier mindset, reduced my stress, and increased my resilience. I was more positive, more optimistic. Every experience was an opportunity for a lesson.

Not only that, but this new, more positive perspective helped me to deal with problems when they arose. Once I truly believed my end would be better than my beginning, I could approach obstacles with an open mind. I could think flexibly and overcome challenges much more effectively. Even if life didn't become easier, my outlook made it easier to deal with.

Part IV

Do you remember that episode of *Martin* where Martin is trying to find topics for his radio show, so Gina comes up with the idea to talk about how they met? If you weren't a fan of the show or don't remember this particular episode, everyone who was at the party where they met has a different recollection of exactly what happened. As they take turns telling the story, everyone tries to make themselves look better.

Gina remembers Martin as a shy nerd. Martin recalls that he wowed Gina by playing the saxophone as he came into the party. Similar to Martin and Gina, depending on who tells it, the story of how my husband and I met varies based on who tells it.

The undisputable part of the story is that we met at church. I had become a consistent 9:30 service member. Going at 9:30 allowed me to help with Children's Church at 11:30 some Sundays . . . I was no longer rushing out the door to get back to bed or brunch. We made eye contact when I went up to pay my offering.

My husband likes to say that since I paid my tithes that day, I left blessed. As I remember things, we made eye contact twice: once when I paid my offering, and then again as we exited church. It was raining, so I recall rushing to my car. I sat there for a second before turning the key in the ignition, and that pause before pulling off is what gave Quavon an opportunity to get my attention.

If it's me telling the story, he banged on my window, startling me. If he tells it, he knocked lightly, and I rolled the window down instantly, smiling from ear to ear. The truth about the specific details of how we met may be a distant memory, but the fact of that Sunday morning in December remains.

We met and exchanged numbers, and when I pulled out of the parking lot, I was excited. I knew there was something special about him. Maybe it was the spark people talk about when they meet the love of their life, but I somehow knew he would be a part of my life.

He called that same afternoon, not long after we met. He called; he didn't text me "Good morning" or "WYD" day after day. He didn't waste my time with a lot of small talk. He called because he wanted to set a date. He wanted to get to know me. He claims that when he called, he got nervous because he heard "a bunch of kids" in the background. Another exaggeration—it was just me and my mom in the kitchen, and anything he heard was the TV.

We planned our first date; I picked the restaurant. At that time, I didn't know what to expect (especially after he told me he was a preacher), and if nothing else came out of our evening together, I knew I would at least have some good Cuban food and leftovers for lunch the next day. I was so anxious before our date. He seemed cool and like lots of fun, but after dating so many of a certain type of guy, the thought of a "church boy" made me laugh. I knew he looked nice in a suit, but what would his everyday clothes look like?

He made reservations for the restaurant I chose, he picked me up on time, and when he got out of the car, he had on Nike boots. He wasn't dressed like a "corny preacher"; I knew he wanted me to notice the Gucci watch on his wrist. I told him I was nervous that he would come dressed like a nerd or a youth pastor. We laughed a lot. We shared a lot.

I learned that although he was a PK (pastor's kid) and had been in church his whole life, he, too, made some choices that could have drastically changed his life. But that was in the past. With a GED and a record, he became the youngest and only Black Financial Center Manager at the Bank of America in our area. He would be graduating in the spring and already had plans to continue on to get his master's. He told me he was surprised I hadn't heard him preach, as he was a guest preacher a couple of times. I admitted if my pastor wasn't going to be there, I would usually stay home.

Our first date was on a Wednesday evening. He surprised me with flowers at my job the very next day. Ironically, his six-year-old son was a student at the school where I was teaching. The card inserted into the flowers read:

Besides theater, musicals, trying different foods, and traveling . . . I hope receiving flowers is also something that you enjoy.

Our next date was that same Saturday. Over the next few weeks, months, and years, we would spend most of our free time together.

We went to plays, watched musicals, tried new restaurants, and traveled together. We both grew in ministry, with him becoming the youth pastor and leader of the young adult ministry. I was over the children's ministry, which had grown from a few children here and there to almost two hundred on Easter Sundays.

He would tease me and say I stopped going to the club when I met him, but the truth is, if I hadn't begun to change my outlook and how I spent my weekends before I met him, I likely wouldn't have been ready for someone like him. I began to accept that I was deserving of good things and that good things could and would last.

I won't say that our relationship was always perfect. Both of us brought with us all of who we were—all our past mistakes, insecurities, and baggage—but we also respected one another. We took the time to get to know each other and learn who we both are individually and as a team. We learned to communicate. I learned how to think before I reacted. He learned to listen. Through it all, we had fun. It may sound cliché, but I married my best friend. He is truly my person.

Part V

Quavon and I got married on April 16, 2016, after about three years of dating. Our wedding day was beautiful. The weather was perfect; the ceremony and reception were filled with so much love. Our families enjoyed each other. I still look at our pictures and smile. My great aunt, who was ninety-two years old at the time, said it was the best wedding she had ever been to, a compliment that continues to bring me joy.

We got wed in April, I graduated with my sixth-year degree in educational leadership in May, and Quavon was ordained in June. Everything was happening so fast. Everything we talked about was coming to be. I started to think more and more about becoming a mother, but after a miscarriage, those old feelings of doubt, guilt, and shame began to resurface.

When that happened, my period was late, and I found out we had miscarried before I had any feelings of hope or excitement that we had conceived a child. In August, I decided to face whatever was going on with my body. I made an appointment with my OB-GYN to follow up with the PCOS and see if anything had changed over ten years later.

My doctor suggested that I have an ultrasound done. I remember laying there as the tech rubbed the cold solution over my stomach, now used to receiving bad news whenever I was in a room that looked like that. I was shocked when she told me there was no evidence of polycystic ovaries and it was clear that I ovulated normally. She even said she wouldn't be surprised if she saw me again soon. My period was due the very next week, and after waiting another week, I finally built up the courage to take a pregnancy test.

I literally laughed out loud at the positive pregnancy test. I took another to be sure. Positive. I immediately took a picture to send to Quavon. I couldn't even focus long enough to think of a creative way to share this news. I just sent the tests. I called the doctor to make an appointment, and despite my excitement, they wouldn't even see me for another four weeks to be sure it was a "viable" pregnancy. So, here I was again, holding on to something that I didn't know how to share. I didn't want to tell my mom . . . yet. I was scared—not for the same reasons that my eighteen-year-old self was, but afraid to get anyone's hopes up.

I held on to the ultrasound pictures from my confirmed pregnancy for about two weeks before I finally just showed them to my mom. In tears, I told her I didn't want to tell her until I knew we would be okay. She looked at me with the same love and affection that she always had and confidently assured me that we would be okay, and I believed her.

I didn't share our news with anyone besides my parents until Thanksgiving, although somehow, my grandfather knew. He would tease me every time he saw me. "I guess you'll tell us on the holiday," he would say. I don't know how he knew, but he did, and in retrospect, I am glad he did because the longer he knew, the longer he had to celebrate the news and think about becoming a great-grandpa.

Throughout my whole pregnancy, I countered my worry with what God had promised me. Yes, I was told that conceiving a baby would be hard and that carrying full-term may also be a challenge. Yes, I had miscarried once before, BUT He would give me beauty for ashes. My ending would be better than my beginning.

I had a pretty routine pregnancy until twenty-eight weeks, when my doctor referred me to a specialist because our baby was "measuring small." I was considered high-risk for the remainder of my pregnancy, and I remember tearing up every time I heard her little heartbeat or when she would flash her hand in front of her face during an ultrasound. Every time they would say how much she weighed, I would always follow with, "But she's okay, right?" I avoided Facebook and pregnancy talk because I often felt ashamed that my body may not be giving my baby what she needed.

On May 5, 2017, I went to my final doctor's appointment. They decided that I would be induced at thirty-nine weeks and told me to expect a call that Sunday with what time I should head to the hospital. We lived about an hour from my hometown and the hospital where I would deliver, so I made plans to go home, rest, and prepare to return sometime on Sunday.

I was visiting with a friend when my mom called to tell me that my grandfather had been taken to the hospital. It appeared he had suffered a heart attack but was coherent and seemed okay. I listened to what she was saying, said a quick prayer, and returned to planning for the arrival of our baby girl.

When they said he would likely be in the hospital for a few days, I mentally adjusted my plan and decided that we would come to New Haven earlier on Sunday so I could spend some time with him before they called to induce me. Then, depending on how long he would spend in the hospital, I would bring the baby to his wing so he could meet her.

That Sunday, my husband and I were walking back to the car after I accompanied him to give communion to an older member of our church, and his phone rang. I was surprised to see it was my mom calling him; I had made sure to keep my ringer on since we were waiting for the call from the hospital to let us know a bed was ready for us. I could tell by his face that whatever my mother told him wasn't good.

"WHY DID SHE CALL YOU?" I asked.

He responded, "He didn't make it."

I felt like the wind had been knocked out of me. I didn't even have the balance to hold myself up. My husband picked me and my nine-month-pregnant belly off the floor of the parking garage. I didn't get there. I didn't get to see him. How could this happen? My grandfather always showed up for me. How could I not show up for him?

Our number one fan, our biggest supporter. Every dance recital, mock trial, debate—he never missed anything. When he shed tears at my graduations, I would beam with pride. He was so proud of me. He really loved me, and in the days leading up to his last moments, I wasn't there.

I don't remember the ride from the hospital in Danbury to our house. I vaguely remember my mom calling back to let me know they were waiting for me there at the hospital so I could see him. Imagine that—my plan was to go see him before I went to the maternity wing, but this wasn't at all how I envisioned it.

I prayed every single night when I was pregnant that my daughter would know her great-grandfather. I literally begged God to let him be a part of her life, and he took his last breath the same day she was scheduled to take her first. I got the call that we should be at Labor and Delivery at 6:30 p.m.

The nurse on the line encouraged me to have a good dinner and get some rest. I needed a moment, but it seemed like there was none. Everything was happening so fast. The worst day I ever had and what would likely be the best day of my life were colliding, and it felt like I wasn't living it but instead watching scenes from a very sad and unbelievable movie.

At my last appointment, they projected she would weigh five pounds, but after nine and a half hours, two epidurals, and a C-section, my beautiful baby came out weighing just over four pounds. She came into this world little and loud. Before I even saw her face, I heard the doctor call her beautiful, then add, "And FIESTY!" They brought her as close to my face as possible, then whisked her away to the NICU.

There were so many concerns for a baby her size, but despite what "they" said, we knew from the beginning she was perfect. I was diagnosed with postpartum preeclampsia. The doctors initially assumed my blood pressure was high because of Papa's passing, but when it didn't go down after delivery or in the days immediately after, I couldn't be released.

I honestly don't know if it was really a condition or if my blood pressure wouldn't go down because my heart wouldn't let me leave my baby. So, we stayed in the hospital for seven days. I didn't get to experience skin-to-skin until the third day, and after helping to write Papa's obituary, I had a pep talk with my little baby. I looked into her big, beautiful eyes and told her she had to get her weight up so we could go home. She looked up at me and confirmed with those same eyes that she understood.

The next day, even with the doctors saying they would likely need to monitor her growth for another week, she was able to nurse, which helped to jumpstart my milk supply. She was eating on her own, off the feeding tube; her body temperature had regulated; and the only thing left was for her to pass the car seat test. I know my baby knew we were proud of her. I think back to that day, and she looked at me the same way she looks at me now when she wants my reassurance that she did something well.

Intrauterine growth restriction (IUGR) is what they say is the cause for Eden's low birth weight. Healthy in every way, my favorite description came from my doctor: "She's perfectly fine. She just may never be a runway model." But if you know my Eden, she will be whatever she wants to be. She was made out of love and born to give back to our family the love we felt we lost the day before her birth.

That's the thing about God: He will always provide—not just physical needs but guidance, strength, comfort, blessings, and sustenance. When you are at your worst, He is at His best, and if you just trust and believe that He is in control, anything is possible—even peace in the midst of the greatest storm. Thankfully, God gave us our greatest blessing in our deepest sorrow, and she is a walking, talking reminder of what love is. We both were released from the hospital on Sunday, May 14, 2017, which was Mother's Day, and she remains the greatest Mother's Day Gift I could ever receive.

My grandfather's funeral was the next day.

As we awaited the limousine to bring us to the church, my grandmother held Eden close. She looked at her and said, "Papa loved you. He loved you so much that he wanted to be the one to usher you into this world. Weeping may endure for a night, but joy cometh in the morning. You are our joy in the morning." And just as they had so many years ago, my grandmother's words permeated through me in a way they had never before:

"The Lord is good; His mercy endures forever, and His faithfulness continues to all generations."

Ashley Newton

Chapter 9

I Obeyed: Connective Tissue

I would like to dedicate my chapter to my "Why", my Northern Stars:

Jacqueline Koonce, Samiyah Lynnice, Justin Bryant, Tahsheika Nazaire, and my Four Fluffy Frenchies (Future, Ciara, Blue, and Smokey the Bear).

Lewis Bryant, Jr., a representation of unconditional love.

All my family, friends, mentors, and advocates.

A special thank you to Queen Latifah and Ms. Rita Owens (Rest In Peace) for encouraging my light to shine bright.

A special thank you to Keema Leyakatalie and Stanley Gabart, who believed in my business when they had access and could have chosen any certified public accountant in the world. You both changed the trajectory of my path in helping others in the entertainment space.

A special thank you to Kato Muhammad.

In memory of, and a special thank you to, the late greats: Rheuben Parramore, Jr.; the legendary Tora Loretta Bell; and my aunt, Ruthie Parramore.

I want to start by saying thank you. Thank you for purchasing this book and reading this chapter. My prayer is that my words and experience will help motivate at least one person to

213

pursue the life they have dreamed of, to never give up, and to always give GOD the glory. My story is about how being obedient and in tune with God's divine ideas and thoughts allowed me to help others and others to help me align with purpose.

The Art of Obeying

If I reflect on how I would want someone to describe me, I would want someone to think, "Lah is intelligent; she is kindhearted; she loves her family; she is active in the community; she is a giving person; she lights up the room with her smile and good energy; she is ethical, loyal, compassionate, professional, driven, best in class, and obedient to God." I wouldn't want someone to say I was religious . . . I don't think of myself as a religious person.

I spent the majority of my life, over twenty-five years, studying every major religion, spiritual manifestation, and the universal law of attraction, and you want to know my takeaway? Ninety-five percent of the information is the same, applied differently; the wordplay is different, but the ideology is the same. I feel that the title of religion, spiritual manifestation, or the Universe (which I believe represents the Holy Spirit or active force of God) moves the focus away from God and more toward man's interpretation of what God wants . . . when all along, God created us in His image, which means we just need to tap into, lean into, what God has placed inside us . . . and this is where all the answers are.

What does it mean to obey? And why is obeying such an important component of submitting your life, your free will, to

God? Why does it matter when you obey? The Merriam-Webster dictionary defines obeying as "1) to follow the commands or guidance of" and "2) to conform to or comply with." Further, the intransitive verb of obey means "to behave obediently." God's favor requires obedience. Spiritually, there is an ocean full of scriptures that discuss obedience.

If we look in the Holy Quran, Surah An-Nisa 4:59 states:

"O you who have believed, obey Allah and obey the Messenger and those in authority among you. And if you disagree over anything, refer it to Allah and the Messenger, if you should believe in Allah and the Last Day. That is the best [way] and best result."

And this is believing—obeying God, his messenger, and those in authority.

If we look into the Bible, 2 John 1:16 states:

"And this is love, that we walk according to His commandments; this is the commandment, just as you have heard from the beginning, so that you should walk in it."

And this is love—honoring a commandment from God.

One of my favorite quotes in the spiritual manifesto
Tao Te Ching says:

"Simplicity, patience, compassion.

These three are your greatest treasures.

Simple in actions and thoughts, you return to the source of being.

Patient with both friends and enemies,

you accord with the way things are.

Compassionate toward yourself,

you reconcile all beings in the world."

Compassion—stepping outside of yourself—humbling yourself, quieting your thoughts to hear divine thoughts and divine ideas.

Growing up, I wouldn't classify myself as an obedient child; I was pretty much the opposite. I was a rebel, always challenging the authority of everyone—everyone except my older sister, Tahsheika, who has the most beautiful name I have ever heard and is the most beautiful person, inside and out, I have ever met to this day. My older sister is a gentle, kind, and loving person; she always showed me compassion through my inquisitive nature. Anything she said went, but everyone else would have a challenge coming to them. I never viewed this "skill" as disrespect; to me, it was my way of communicating, understanding, gathering information, and analyzing.

I loved analyzing everything and counting—counting *everything*. I would walk into rooms and count every object several times, often while people were talking—which, coupled with challenging them, didn't go over too well. Gratefully, I also have a mother who allowed me to be me and evolve into the woman I am today. My mother was always happy, carefree, fun-loving, always nurturing everyone in our circle of life, and patient. I could count on one hand how many times she was angry or sad.

216

Most children growing up would be afraid of not following the rules. I lived to challenge rules and all those in authority of those rules. I decided that if I couldn't get the person in authority to see and understand my perspective, I was okay with the punishment or outcome. Long story short: Obedience is not a word that resonated in my aura, which meant many days of punishment and after-school detention . . .

. . . until I was backstage holding hands with a legend in the music industry as they began to pray before their sold-out arena show (over 30,000 people).

As they prayed, they said, "Thank You, God, for everyone who obeyed You on my behalf." Then, The Legend squeezed my hand, looked me in my eyes, and said, "You did this, Ms. Lah. You did all of this. Your obedience and connective tissue did all of this."

My response? "Not me! Give all the glory to God!" The favor of God.

The Legend said, "Look how God uses people!"

The next day, she called me and said, "Ms. Lah, I would like for you to accompany me on my private jet as we travel to the next location so we can discuss how I want to change elements of the show." When I boarded the private jet, I had to hold back tears for a variety of reasons, but the key reason was that God allowed me to accomplish something like this on my terms with His guidance and direction, walking with integrity, with Him using people who obeyed on my behalf.

People say, "God will put your name in rooms of people that you don't even know." I can tell you I am a testimony of that. I have had clients call me and say, "So-and-so referred you. You come highly recommended." I want EVERYBODY TO KNOW "*BUT GOD!*" I don't want to ever forget "*BUT GOD!*" During this time, life was happening to me all at once. Have you ever felt like taking a time-out? Just wanting to press a time-out button and rest, like, "Let me pause life real quick"? When nothing appears to be flowing, when you continue to pour into life, and life is like, "So? Give me more!" and you just want to run away or take a long nap, like hibernation, I'm here to tell you that you are not alone. I have felt that several times during my life journey. What I have learned is not to complain. Praise. Speak life over your life. It took me forty-six years to understand the importance of this.

Below are a couple of my favorite scriptures when I just feel like running away from life, when things aren't working out according to how I think the plan should go. I prayerfully remind God and myself of the promises that can not fail:

> » 1 Peter 5:7 — Cast all your anxieties on Him because He cares for you.
> » Romans 8:28 — And we KNOW that for those who love God, all things work together for good, for those who are called according to His purpose.
> » Isaiah 54:17 — NO weapon formed against you shall prosper, and you will succeed, and every tongue that rises against you in judgment you will condemn.

» 2 Timothy 1:7 — For God gave us a spirit not of fear but of power, love, and sound mind.

» Philippians 4:6 — Be anxious for nothing, but in everything, by prayer and supplication with thanksgiving, let your requests be made known to God.

» 1 John 5:14 — This is the confidence that we have in Him that if we ask anything according to His will, He hears us.

Remember: "The chaos around you shouldn't override the calm within you."

To continue (backstage, prayer, and The Legend), during this time, I was still suffering from debilitating depression because my dear hero father committed suicide in February 2021. He was such a great father and a mentally strong person; now, I realize how much a person could be hurting inside or feeling overwhelmed by life. He called me the day prior to committing suicide, and I missed his call. I tried to call him back that day but couldn't reach him. He had spoken with my three other sisters, and they all called me, saying, "Dad said to call him." I told my sisters that I had called him back and would call him again in the morning. Around 4:00 a.m., I woke up extremely sad. The first thing I went to do was call my dad, but because of the time, I said to myself, *If you call him now, he will think it's an emergency and it may worry him, so wait.* So, I said to myself, *I'll just call him first thing in the morning.* Then, another thought came to me: *What if he isn't there in the morning? What if something is wrong?* Then, I began to cry and pray, asking God to not let anything be wrong; I would call him first thing in the morning.

I got up at around 8:00 a.m. and called my dad. He didn't answer, so I left a long voicemail telling him how much I loved him and to call me back. As soon as I hung the phone up, my youngest sister called me and said, "I'm sorry. Dad is gone. He killed himself." I was just devastated. I didn't believe it—to the point that I hired a private investigator to investigate my dad's death.

One of the last things that he said to my middle sister the night before was that anything bad that may have happened to us in life was because he wasn't by our side; he wasn't there for us. That comment resonates with the little girl in me; however, I never thought my dad wasn't there for me—in fact, I felt the total opposite. He was potentially torturing himself with thoughts that were not aligned with how we, or I, felt. Just super sad.

About a week after his passing, *Billboard* announced the top business managers of 2021, and I—little old me—was on the list. My dad named me Lateefah Parramore. I feel like I have such a cool name for what I do; I wasn't named after Queen Latifah or the band Paramore, but they are two of my favorite entertainers. I remember I began to cry, wishing my dad was alive to see my name in *Billboard*—the name he gave me, Lateefah Parramore. We don't realize how much people suffer in silence, and I made a commitment to do better at checking in on family and friends.

My favorite person, Aunt Loretta, Tora Loretta Bell, passed away of a massive heart attack in January 2022. She was the reason I became a CPA, and in 2023, I was in the midst of a relationship breakup of three and a half years. We had just purchased a multi-million dollar home that I now needed to move out of and sell—

and, just like that, I was homeless, or displaced, living in an Airbnb until the house sold. *How did I become homeless, or displaced, with four dogs and all of our possessions in storage or in my G-Wagon? Displaced with a car that costs over $200,000 is insane.* I was clearly insane. Don't get me wrong—of course, I could have moved back with my mother, but she was three hours away from my business home base.

A week prior to the prayer, as I was driving down the highway on my way to meet my realtor to find a place to live, I got a call from this aforementioned legend. I was reluctant to answer the phone because 1) I don't answer calls from numbers I do not know and 2) I literally had tears in my eyes, feeling extremely overwhelmed by my personal circumstances, yet still striving for perfection. I answered the phone a bit down, and, feeling sorry for myself, I answered.

"Hello?"

The Legend said, "Hi! I am The Legend, and I would like to speak to Ms. Parramore. My attorney was going to call you, but I wanted to call you because I have researched you and I want to be your client. I'll be your best client."

My mouth was on the floor.

The Legend continued, "My tour starts this week, and I would like to meet you at the first stop so we can do business together."

Of course, I agreed. We met, I heard them and what they wanted, I made it happen, and the rest is history. Most people talk, pontificate, and create theories. I strategically plan and do. I do.

One of my favorite clients is an indie record label. The indie label has a significant and consistently successful track record of finding new artists, developing them, and breaking them, creating number one trending songs and multi-millionaires. I always loved watching the process. I normally wouldn't have any input in creative artistry—just finances, the money.

One day, I was visiting the recording studio, and I met a beautiful young lady who was extremely passionate about her catalog of songs. She said, "Ms. Lah, listen to my album." So, I went into the recording studio and started to listen. I was loving every song, and just watching her excitement made me feel a connection. Her face would light up with excitement as she sang her songs, then she would perform the songs in the studio space as if she was in front of twenty thousand people. That's a star—unique, authentic star quality. I listened for hours, asking the engineer to rewind. She would get excited and perform the part of the song again and again as if I was hearing it for the first time. At the end of the session, I looked at her and told her she was going to be a superstar.

Upon leaving, I immediately called the owner of the indie label. I told him about the session, sharing that I thought she was a superstar, and they needed to focus on pushing her as an artist. The owner agreed—"Lah, that's the plan!"—and the rest is history. Six months later . . . several chart-topping songs later . . . the indie label was having a birthday party for the artist. I walked up to her and congratulated her on all the recent success.

She looked at me with a tear in her eye and said, "Ms. Lah, you played a huge part in this success." She continued, "They told me that you called them and were so passionate about my project that it motivated them to push me hard. I want to thank you."

I smiled. I was and am so happy for her. I said, "It's all God. Praise God." It was God's idea that told me to call. Normally, I stay in my money lane. I went outside of the box because I obeyed.

Recently, a young lady, about thirteen years old, said something. She spoke a word over her life circumstance that I have to share: Her mother suffered from a life-threatening disease and was hospitalized for months. During that time, her mother had four surgeries; they lost their home and all material possessions (because they didn't have any family in the U.S.); and they had to move with a friend, who treated them horribly. After nine months, God put them on the heart of the president of their country, and he made calls, trying to find them. When he found them, he made sure the mom had proper medical care, gave the mom a job, and facilitated a home for them; essentially, God used the president to restore their life, making it ten times better than it was nine months prior. The thirteen-year-old said, "If only I knew that season was only going to be nine months. I would have praised God instead of complaining the entire time."

But God . . . If only we knew how long our "season" was because that's what it is: a season. A lesson, not a loss; a season, not a lifetime. So, whatever season you are in, chin up and praise Him! You've got this, and God's got you!

After the prayer backstage, I got chills watching The Legend perform. It was early 2023, and it hit me . . . I finally understood the importance of obeying or listening and acting in alignment with the divine thought or divine idea that you receive for the benefit of others. I mean, I knew I had a divine gift and would receive divine thoughts and ideas to help others, but this was the first time someone actually put it in words. Ms. Lah was obedient on God's behalf, and now, we're here, living the dream. How did I get here? How did I become this person—a person who legends, billionaires, multi-millionaires, and people who influence change in the world listen to? Me . . . little old me. How did I become a high-value human, so to speak? How? I'm just a little girl with a big dream from Newark, New Jersey.

When I look back on my life journey, I think about how my life would have had a different outcome if others were not obedient on my behalf. Where I'm from, living past early twenties is a miracle, which systematically and physiologically caused young adults to live fast. I remember when I was thirteen years old, it was a "red summer"; so many young people died, to the point that my grandmother forbade us from attending any more funerals that summer. I would have easily been a statistic. Obedience equates to God's favor. I also think about how I have impacted the lives of many by being obedient. As my Aunt Ruthie would say, to God be the glory!

Connective Tissue

There's something about how during the moments when I feel beaten up by life, God allows me to use my divine gift for others: His grace and favor, the blessings of discernment and obedience. I pour into people, their careers, their families, and their brands every day, nonstop. Every day, I try to make people feel good; make them feel special; make them feel like their dreams, goals, and aspirations are possible and attainable; and help make it happen, whatever it takes. That work builds connective tissue.

People often ask me how I fell in love with the entertainment business; it was at the age of two years old. I was sitting in the audience in a theater in Newark, New Jersey, with a sippy cup in hand, next to my older sister. We were watching our mother dance on stage. I remember being amazed. I remember thinking, *She must be an angel. She must be Wonder Woman. She must be Superwoman. How can she dance like that?* It was like an out-of-body experience. I remember my entire body feeling every step she made. And I loved when people said my mother's name: Jacqueline "Jackie" Koonce. At that moment, I didn't realize what she was doing, but I knew that it was a gift from God, that it wasn't from a human being.

If you have intimate conversations with most creatives, artists, musicians, etc., they will talk about a physical transition that happens when they create or perform, almost like a download from God. I recall asking my mother to let me count her money. She obeyed. She would let me count her money all day and night. I would play with my imagination, imagining that I was a big-time money guy making deals, helping people, and counting money. She obeyed. She could have easily said, "You are three or four years old. What do you know about money?" But she didn't. She said, "Teefah, every dollar better be there when you bring the money back to me." And it was. Every time. Not a penny missing. My mother would brag about how good I was at counting money and finding money around the house. I vividly remember being backstage and having the confidence to ask other people if they needed me to count their money. Her telling her friends about my "money guy skills" encouraged me in a funny way. Ms. Money Guy . . .

At ten years old, I decided that my career path would be to become the biggest drug dealer from Newark. So, I figured if I held a meeting with the biggest drug dealer on my block that was close to my age, he would mentor me and take me under his wing, and that would be the start of my drug empire. Win-win. I can never forget it; it was a beautiful Friday morning. I woke up early; put on one of my favorite sweatsuits that was gray, pink, and white; a clean pair of sneakers; and a pair of gold earrings; and put my hair in a ponytail. I walked to the corner of South Orange Avenue and Seventh Street, and there he was: PeeWee, twelve years old, one of the most respected corner boys. I didn't realize the positions at the time or the hierarchy of the drug business. I got straight to the point.

I said—with a big, confident smile on my face, mind you— "Good morning, fam. I decided I want to sell drugs, and I want to work with you, not for you, as a start to my empire."

PeeWee had so much swagger. He wasn't the biggest, height- or weight-wise, but he was the most serious. His demeanor was extremely masculine. He was a person of little words, even at the age of twelve. His skin tone was the most striking chocolate I had ever seen in person; it almost glowed. He had "Chinese eyes" and

226

a delicate beauty mark on the right side of his face. He always tilted his head before he spoke.

He leaned up against a fence, put his left leg on the fence, tilted his head to the right, and said, "Lahhhhh, White Bread (that was the nickname my block gave me because I was light-skinned and read the dictionary) . . . Lahhh, nah, you can't be no drug dealer."

My feelings were so hurt. Like, crushed.

I said, "What you mean? I'm tough. I'm smart. I'm good with money. I can do it."

PeeWee said, "Lah, nah. You better than this street life. You are meant to be somebody. You not regular; you are meant to get out of the hood and do good things for this world." He continued, "If you want money, I will flip money for you, but you can't be out here. And I'm gonna tell everybody that if they do business with you, they are going to have to answer to me."

He deflated my dream of being the biggest drug dealer in the world. He obeyed. He spoke life over me. He prophesied over me at the age of twelve, in one of the roughest hoods in the country. God gave him the vision—he obeyed. I left that day extremely discouraged and conflicted. For the first time, I briefly thought about what God wanted for me as opposed to what I wanted for me. What I wanted was MONEY, and A LOT of it. By the age of ten, I had already had two near-death experiences where my life had to be saved, and yet, during those times, I never even thought about why God had saved my life—that I potentially had a purpose if I obeyed.

When I think about my near-death experiences, the same person intervened to save me every time. The first time, my mother was having a birthday party for me and my older sister; my birthday is in June, and hers is in August. An amazing beach birthday party! I didn't know how to swim, but I wanted to play with the big kids and adults. While playing, I was thrown into the deep end of the water. Time legit stopped. It was like a movie. I was yelling for help, and suddenly, I was underwater, not able to get back to the top of the water.

My older sister saw me and said, "Grab my bikini!"

I managed to grab her bikini bottom (still underwater and holding my breath), and she was trying to run toward the shallow end, but I was heavy, and I felt her bikini bottom begin to fall. Just when I felt like I was going to pass out, one of my mother's friends—Earl, whom we called "Big Earl"—grabbed me out of the water and took me to shore. After I calmed down, I made someone teach me how to swim that day. I never wanted anything to have a one-up on me, so to speak.

The second near-death experience occurred at my mother's management/recording studio office, Starship Entertainment. My sister and I normally played with the instruments or in the recording studio, but that day, I wanted to play between the hallway and the office because my mother expanded to the suite adjacent to her original office. It was also late in the evening, around 7 p.m., and all of the other companies in the building had gone for the day. The front entrance of the main office had a glass door, and I was playing around the door—leaning on the glass, running in and out. My mother had just said, "Stop playing on that door." At that moment, the glass broke, and I fell through the glass door. I was stuck in the middle of the glass door, and Big Earl pulled me out just in time. As soon as he pulled me out from between the glass, the last, V-shaped piece of glass headed straight for me and crashed on the floor. If anyone ever saw the movie *Ghost* starring Whoopie Goldberg, visually, it was the same scene where the guy in the movie died. That could have been me. I remember glass was everywhere—I still have scars on my lower back as a reminder of that evening. A handful of years later, PeeWee was one of the biggest sergeants in the South Orange Avenue Posse (SOAP) and drug game, and he was murdered at the age of sixteen. I couldn't attend his funeral because by this time, my mother had obeyed and moved us to Florida.

I often think about that day and PeeWee. I think about how his life may have been different if someone had spoken about God's life, a divine thought, or a divine idea over him.

At the age of twelve years old, I had an encounter that would change the way I viewed my name. My name is Arabic, and I had never met another Lateefah in my entire twelve years of living. My mother always had multiple streams of income. She was an executive assistant at Irvington High School's alternative night school. Most days, after school, my sister and I would go from our middle school to Irvington High School to spend the evening with our mother while she worked. I loved going to her office because she would allow me to type on her typewriter and use all of her office supplies. It was a dream made in Heaven. I would walk through the halls and see all the awards of the high school's star athletes. One of the most famous was Queen Latifah. I would study her awards in amazement because I was not athletic at all.

One evening, I was typing on the typewriter typing a bunch of nothing; my mother was reviewing schedules of the teenagers, and my sister was reading and reviewing her schoolwork. All of a sudden, the office door swung open, and this fly ass woman came through the door. My jaw dropped. She was dressed in black leather from head to toe, with a plush black leather jacket and gloves; beautiful dangling gold earrings; a black kufi hat that sat on her head like a crown; and long, healthy, golden-brown hair that looked freshly pressed. I had the habit of freezing when I got excited. In my mind, I was like, *Is that Queen Latifah?*

The woman said, "Ms. Koonce, have you seen my mother?"

My mother responded, "Dana! So great to see you. No, I haven't seen your mother."

The woman's mother, Ms. Rita Owens, was a teacher at the high school and taught at the alternative school in addition to teaching during the day.

My mother continued, "Let me introduce you to my daughters."

Queen Latifah responded, "Ms. Koonce, they are beautiful!"

My mother said, gesturing to me and my sister, "This is Iesha, and that is Lateefah."

Queen Latifah and I looked at each other and smiled.

She said, "Ms. Koonce, I love their names." She continued, "Iesha . . . that means alive—that's a beautiful name. But . . . Lateefah . . . Lateefah—intelligent and kind. With that name, you are going to go far. You are going to be something special. Mark my words."

And, just like that, she spoke a divine plan over my life. I was still frozen. I unfroze just enough to shake her hand. I look back on that encounter, and my heart is always warmed thinking about how divine the moment was. Throughout my life, when I would introduce myself, people would always say, "Lateefah? Like Queen Latifah?" and I would say, "Yes—exactly like Queen Latifah."

Upon graduating high school, my favorite aunt, the legendary Tora Loretta Bell, was newly released from federal prison after serving a full sentence of eight years for being one of the most notorious women in the drug game. She was on the alphabet boys' most wanted list, with a reward in the multimillion-dollar range. I remember visiting her in prison over the years. It looked like a college campus with dorms; she always kept her spirits up and made lifelong friends there.

I always wanted to be like her. She was no-nonsense, sharp, intelligent, fearless, stylish—just a leader and boss. I looked up to her for so many reasons, the number one reason being that she was always her authentic self and said it like it was at all times. You never wanted to be on the opposite side of hers—just be prepared. She was extremely well-read and well-traveled. She had so many stories, so many catchphrases, for every life situation. If I was sad over a breakup, she would say, "You know what they say: You get over one by getting under another, Niecey-poo." Then, she would let out a hearty, soulful laugh, and I would join her. When she came to visit me in Miami to handle the money at the door for an event I was hosting, she told a person who was disrespectful, "I didn't come here to fight, but I will." She looked at me, and we both laughed in a sinister way. I was her favorite, as well. She let everyone know that.

I sure do miss her . . . I miss her every day. Her voice was a deep, sultry sound—methodical. In college, my major was sales and marketing. I didn't know what to major in, so I picked sales, although my passion was MONEY!!! I figured sales would turn into money. After school one day, I went to my Aunt Loretta's house and told her that I didn't like my major.

She said, "You know, Niecey-poo, I always saw you handling money and doing business with money. You need to be an accountant, then a CPA." She continued, "You know, a CPA is a certified public accountant. It's like a doctor or lawyer in accounting; you have to take an exam harder than the bar exam."

I listened intently as she continued.

"You know, I wanted to be a CPA. But now, with federal time on my jacket, I could never be a CPA, but you can."

She smiled, then I smiled.

I said, "Then, I'll be a CPA for us!" We both smiled and hugged.

She would always end every conversation with, "Good enough," "You know I love you," or both. The next day, I changed my major to accounting and started researching what a CPA was because I had no idea a job like that even existed. I still had no idea what a CPA actually did. When people think of an accountant, they think of taxes. I didn't want to be a tax practitioner. I wanted to do something else . . . something fun! My aunt obeyed, and I listened. I truly believe that she received a divine idea that day and communicated it to me. Another conversation changed my life path, a life of which the foundation is built upon helping people build their wealth profiles—their real wealth profiles.

After graduating from college, my first stop in my professional career was as an accounting team member at the prestigious Ernst & Young LLP. I remember the forms I had to complete about my family background and the VHS video tapes they made us watch—literally called "The Firm," it was a whole new world that I stepped into. Like most people of color, we don't necessarily have people in our families with a legacy of a specific career experience. The dinner table wasn't filled with discussions about financial matters, mental health, life expansion, etc. I never even met a CPA until my third year of college through the National Association of Black Accountants, Inc. The extended family that I met along my journey has always advocated the mantra, "Lifting as we climb." I always felt a sense of family, that I wasn't alone. There were significant hurdles and challenges, and I reached an extensive level of personal fortitude. During my career at Ernst & Young, I was afforded mentors and advocates who obeyed and helped facilitate my career success. One mentor, Greg Collins, would show me the blueprint of the entertainment business: what it takes to be best in class and core skills to survive and thrive as a woman. I took the knowledge and perfected my craft.

Throughout my career, I have broken boundaries. I received accolades, such as the first African American woman to receive the Florida Institute of Certified Public Accountants's Woman to Watch award, a feature in *Variety* magazine as a trusted advisor, and recognition as one of *Billboard* magazine's top business managers. With all the awards and accolades, I can never forget those throughout my life who obeyed and helped me or spoke a word over my life. In Psalm 23, David said, "The Lord is my shepherd. I shall not want." He didn't say, "I shall not need." Needs are a given. He said, "I shall not WANT." God provides all things good—our needs and wants. It's law: Thou shall not WANT.

On this journey, I have perfected my craft, worked consistently and diligently, and remained dedicated to the mission. The mission: Use my God-given talent, obeying God, divine ideas, and divine thoughts to help passionate creatives, artists, and entertainers elevate their crafts. I always felt that my ideas or strategy were not from me but sort of like downloads. Early in the mornings, from around 3 a.m. to 6 a.m., I would wake up with divine ideas for someone. I would write them down and begin strategically developing a plan of execution. It could be a current client or a potential client; the ideas would just flow. People always say I have amazing energy and that my energy is electrifying. I have come to realize that that's not me, either. I feel the positive flow of the energy is the Holy Spirit working on God's behalf because, low-key, I am an introvert. I have anxiety when interacting with people. So, it has to be God. I have been blessed to have godly encounters.

When I think about it, there were so many people throughout my journey who obeyed, which is why I live my life striving for obedience. We are all connected, and when we use those connections to be a steward of our gifts and pour into others, we build connective tissue. I always knew I would be rich. It wasn't until I submitted my will to God's will over my life, asked to be His friend, and made clear my intentions to be a servant that made His heart rejoice that I became wealthy.

Lah Real Wealth, a.k.a. Ms. Money Guy.

Lateefah Parramore

Chapter 10

BENT BUT NOT BROKEN

Dedicated to my children, grandchildren, and Mom.

"You can never compare Eric to Rico because that is like comparing champagne to beer," my ex-husband whispered in my ear out of nowhere.

Eric was my ex-husband's nephew, and Rico was our son. *Wow. How can you say that about our son?* I thought. I was in active labor, laying on a hospital bed at the time, birthing our second son into this world. The act of giving birth brings women to the doorstep of death; anything could happen. It is one of the most vulnerable times of a woman's life. With all of the risks, it is also the most rewarding act that I ever experienced.

Being in labor is a memorable moment for any mother, yet he didn't want to see me happy. He uttered hateful things to me in an attempt to steal my joy. His tactics worked, and my heart broke a little, but I decided to shift my focus to having a successful delivery. My ex-husband constantly tried to tear me down and break my spirit, but God's favor always comforted me. I am Cheryl Mutcherson, and this is my story.

I was born on February 17, 1958, to Ollie and Ollie Mae Mutcherson. I am the eldest of three siblings, Anthony, Andrea, and Sonia Mutcherson. My childhood life was great, but it would take a major turn when I became a teenager. My ninth-grade year would be a life-changing experience, for this is when I would meet Mick. He was my worst nightmare.

Mick was handsome, charming, and a smooth talker. I was walking down my street one evening when a car pulled up beside me, and in the back seat sat this well-dressed, good-looking guy (Mick). To my amazement, he was an arrogant, egotistical, self-centered manipulator. My friend, who was like an uncle or big brother to me, was driving the vehicle. My friend would talk me into going on a date with Mick—which really would not be a date because he went off talking to other people at the football game. I should have known what type of boyfriend he would be by his actions on this date.

I came to know Mick a little better, and he wasn't so bad of a person—and, much to my surprise, he asked my parents if he could court me. That's how it was done back in my day: The boy asked the girl's parents if he could date her or have her hand in marriage. My parents actually said yes, and I was very surprised because I had never dated or courted before. Mick could only court me in the presence of one of my parents, at our home.

The courtship would only last for my ninth-grade year because Mick's grandmother would send him back to his mother in New York after she found out that he had been skipping school. Mick would keep in touch by calling and writing to me from New York. He would visit every summer, and the courtship would continue, but little did I know, being so naive, he had other girlfriends in NYC.

The summer of my senior year would change my life forever. It would be this summer that I would be accused by my mother of having sex. I would, out of spite, let Mick go all the way. I was a virgin, and my mother was saying I was having sex when I had not been touched by a male. It was my first time, and I hated every minute of the sex. This is how it all started: He talked me into visiting him at his grandmother's house. His grandmother was out of town. I went over to visit him, he asked me to come to his bedroom, and he was lying in bed. This was the day my virginity was stolen.

I wondered what the hype was all about with sex because it wasn't all that for me. Afterward, I hated him and what he had done to me. He violated my body and hurt it; therefore, I wanted nothing else to do with him. I would not talk to him for a while. I didn't want to see or hear from him. My uncle asked me if it was that bad. My answer was yes. This sex thing was not what I had been told.

I would later have to speak with Mick because I would find out I was pregnant. I had conceived; now, I had to talk to him. This was not what I had planned or expected nor what I wanted. A baby was not in my plans for a long time, especially as a teenager. *Oh, my God. What have I done?* I was devastated.

I didn't know I was pregnant until my mother told me. She had been checking my period every month. I had irregular periods (meaning they did not come on every month). The worst part of it all was that my mom told my dad. *How could she do this to me? How could I do this to myself?* My father had the audacity to ask me how I liked the sex. Oh, boy, was I embarrassed.

I can remember it like it was a few minutes ago. My little sister, Sonia, was hiding underneath the table, listening to our conversation. I almost threw up. We were having dinner, and only the two of us were left at the table, with the little eavesdropper underneath the table. *Oh, my God.* Could things get any more awkward? My dad asked how I enjoyed sex, and my little sister was listening underneath the table. I was supposed to set a good example for my little sister, and this was not a good look. I wanted to gag. What would you have done in this situation?

I just wanted to curl up into a knot and die. My life was over as I knew it. All I could say to myself was, *This, too, shall pass sooner than later.* I would've preferred it to pass right then. The embarrassment would pass, but much to my surprise, that would not be the end of my dismay.

I didn't think the whole world would know of my pregnancy soon. I could not imagine showing my face at school. What would my peers say? ("This seventeen-year-old virgin is pregnant!") I wanted to scream, "God, PLEASE TAKE THIS HEAVY BURDEN AND PAIN AND NIGHTMARE AWAY FROM ME," but instead, all I could pray was, "God, be with me, and let Your will be done in my baby's life and my life. Please forgive me for my sins."

To add salt to my wound, my church wanted me to stand in front of the congregation to ask for their forgiveness for getting pregnant out of wedlock. I told my mother I refused because it was between God and myself. The Bible stated that if a woman is pregnant and not married, she must go before the church and ask for forgiveness. I had already gone before God and my parents, and they were the only ones I needed forgiveness from. *WOW!!!* Adding insult to injury. *How could this have happened to me my first time having sex? I've hurt my mother, father, brother, and sister—not counting God, as well. What have I done?!*

I learned a very valuable lesson: Do not try to hurt other people, for you will only get hurt in the end being spiteful. I found myself in this situation because my mom thought I was sexually active, and I was not. To hurt her, I had sex . . . I hurt myself trying to hurt her. I paid a big price and learned a valuable lesson for being disobedient. Listen to your mothers and everyone who imparts wisdom into your life; it is not to harm you but to help you.

Mick would go back to New York City after the summer was over. My mom said I had to get him and his mom on the phone to tell them I was pregnant with his child. My mother broke the news to him and his mother. He and his family were very supportive; everyone was all hands on deck. His uncle wanted me and the baby to move to Boston with him and his wife; of course, my mother said no. They were willing to send me to Boston University and help with the baby. Later, his uncle would always be a big help to me and the baby.

My mother and I both had big plans for me. I wanted to go into basic training and join the Air Force to become the first Black female pilot. I could have still joined the Air Force, but would later turn them down because I thought I would have to give my son up to a family member. I misunderstood the recruiter; he only meant that I would have to let a relative keep him until I completed basic training.

For my high school graduation, my mother had to save money to buy me a brand-new Pontiac Firebird. I messed that up; now, she said she had to pay for a baby. My mom wanted me to go to college to become a dental hygienist or a physical therapist. A baby was nowhere in my life plans at that time. My life changed in the blink of an eye all due to one big, treacherous mistake.

Mick lured me to his house with one plan in mind: to seduce me and take my virginity—but not to implant me with his seed. I never would have dreamt of being pregnant at seventeen. *This only happens on TV or to other girls, not to me.* This was not my dream at all. What a life-changer for me. I had no idea my mother was checking for my period every month.

Also, my senior year would be the year I would meet a young man who did not care about me being pregnant. We met at his school. He was also a senior but at another high school. My school was being remodeled, and students from my school had to attend his school during the renovation. Tristan would get me whatever I needed or wanted during my pregnancy. He would take me to my doctor's appointments. This was the beginning of a beautiful friendship, even though he wanted to be more than friends. Friendship was all that I could give at the time; I felt that giving more would not be right for him.

He was willing to accept my baby and be his father, but I had to give his biological father a chance. Tristan showed us so much love and affection. I wish I had chosen Tristan back then and let him into my life. He turned out to be a successful businessman, living in NYC. To this day, I sometimes wonder what my life would have been like with Tristan. This was my first string on the bow being bent—and yet, not broken.

The Pregnancy and the Birth

To begin with the pregnancy, my mother let my aunt talk her into sending me to the health department for my prenatal care. I was too out done with my aunt (meaning I was not happy with her suggestion), and she would be the one to take me to my first prenatal appointment. The doctor examined me and did not tell me anything, so when my mother asked me if I was pregnant, I told her no; the doctor never said or told me I was.

My mom said, "Well, your aunt said you are, and the baby is due on May 18, 1976."

I said, "Oh, that's news to me," being smart.

My mother and everyone finally accepted the pregnancy and were there for me—everyone but my little sister. She was angry because she was like my little girl. I am six years older than her. Sonia thought the baby was taking her place in the house. I can remember her jumping up in the middle of the bed, saying, "I hope it dies! I hope it dies!" referring to my baby. She had made a song out of it. Sonia saw all the baby things coming in the house and thought she wasn't the baby anymore, but that was not so. Later, when Rico was born, Sonia would be his biggest fan and protector.

I missed out on the senior trip to Disney because I was nine months pregnant and due to have the baby soon. I missed out on the prom—actually, on the night of the prom, my girlfriends called me from the prom when I was officially in labor. I was having bad pain that felt like cramps.

I thought my stomach was hurting because I was stealing my mom's Mother's Day dinner for the next day. I had eaten too many collard greens. My stomach continued to hurt, and I was home alone with my younger siblings. I called my Aunt Mazie, and she, in turn, asked me if my water broke or if I passed a pink mucus plug. I said I didn't know. She asked me to go into the restroom and wipe myself, and there was the pink mucus plug. She was on her way to take me to the hospital.

My aunt and her friend came; her friend had to drive because my aunt didn't know how to drive. We would then have to stop and get gas on the way to the hospital. A police officer was there, who, in turn, escorted us to the hospital. I got to the hospital to find I'd not dilated enough. The doctor gave me a shot and sent me on my way back home. My mother met us at the hospital.

The nurse was so rude to me because I was so young. She really didn't know my story. She told me, "All you young girls go out having sex and cannot handle having a baby." I was so upset with this nurse. How could she have known it was my first time? All she saw was a pregnant teenage girl. Labor would last another twenty-four hours before I would have a healthy baby boy.

I returned to the hospital on Sunday afternoon like the attending physician required, only to not give birth until 12:57 p.m. the following day. A gift bassinet was being given away to the first mother who delivered closest to midnight on Mother's Day. I didn't make it. My baby did not want to come into this old, sinful world— and yes, you guessed it: The basket went to another mother.

I did not get to see him when he was born because I'd lost too much blood. I had to be packed with gauze. I had complications with the delivery; my pelvis was too small for the baby to come through the birth canal. The doctors prepped me to have the baby, and he stopped coming. I had to be taken down for an X-ray of my pelvis. I'll never forget the young intern who volunteered to take me for an X-ray. I think he was the nicest person in the entire hospital. God favored me to have at least one person to show me kindness during this very difficult time of my life. I felt like everyone was judging me until I met him. I've learned to be kind to any and everyone because you do not know what they are going through and how impactful your actions can be.

I was heavily medicated, and I did not have any recollection of the details of my delivery. My roommate told me everything she saw that happened after we got to know each other. Rico was also born with jaundice, meaning too many of his red blood cells were breaking down. I could not hold him or see him until the next evening. I also had a high fever the night before.

The first time I saw my son, he was a very little, really light baby with light green eyes, and I was afraid of him. He was so tiny. I had three nurses and about two doctors ask if I was going to put him up for adoption. My mother told them, "Absolutely not. This is our baby." They said they wanted to adopt him if we would put him up for adoption. "No, not my baby," I said. My son and I would be released from the hospital and live a good life without his father for a year. Mick would return after a year to meet his son; he only came to Florida during the summer since he was still living with his mom for the school year.

The Marriage

Mick would come back to Florida after a year to see me and his son. Life for me and my son would change drastically. Mick would try to dictate both our lives; he was controlling. The only reason he would return to see us was because his family made him. I didn't need him or his help because I had a support system with my friends and family. My father would tell me I could not live with

Mick; if I did, I could not visit my family. We would have to get married as opposed to living together, so Mick married me.

We didn't tell anyone but my mother. Mick and I got married in my mother's living room, with my sister and brother as witnesses. My neighbor was a minister; he married us. The day we got married, he left me with his aunt and uncle in Orlando, Florida. This was supposed to be our honeymoon, and he went off to be with someone else. I wanted the marriage annulled.

Mick begged, saying he would do better. He was not ready for a baby and definitely not marriage; being tied to someone for a lifetime was simply out of the question for him. A month later, I was pregnant again with our second child. What a boomer. I had gotten an IUD for protection not to get pregnant, and I guess God said another baby was needed to make the marriage work. WRONG!!!

I had been bleeding nonstop for about six weeks. When I visited the doctor, he said, "Congratulations! You are six weeks pregnant, but the bad news is that the baby is trying to abort because of the IUD." He took the IUD out and said, "The baby will abort itself soon, like a regular abortion." Well, much to my suprise, the baby fought to live. I went home to tell Mick, and he said, "I don't want to hear it." *Here I am again, pregnant and married at twenty years old, but at least this time, I'm married. This is just what I need at this time. GREAT. I hate my life, and now, I have another mouth to feed and worry about protecting from this curly man.*

Mick didn't want me to work; he wanted to control every move I made and my whereabouts. I had to ask him for money or whatever I needed, and I was not used to that. He decided if I would need whatever I said I needed or not. I went out and got a job as a maid at the Motel 6—boy, did he hate that. I only worked a month because I was pregnant and the conditions at the motel were bad. A couple of the workers got lice from cleaning the rooms and handling the linens. I told Mick about the incident, and I had to quit.

I can remember going into labor on a Friday night and calling my doctor to inform him of my labor pain. He told me to come to the hospital. I, in turn, told him I would be there on Monday because that's when my baby was due. I was remembering the labor I had with my first child. The doctor asked to speak to my husband. I told him, "I don't care who you speak with. I'm not coming to the hospital until Monday."

I didn't go to the hospital until Monday morning. I remember having a conversation with Mick about timing my contractions, during which he told me, "Time them yourself." I was in disbelief. *WOW! What a stand-up guy!* I kept so much from my family and friends when I should have been telling it all.

When someone tries to isolate you, and/or you feel as though you cannot share the things that they are putting you through, it is time to leave. This is your one precious life—live it to the fullest, and never let anyone keep you from peace and happiness. If you do not know how to leave, seek God's wisdom and ask Him for courage.

Why did my son and I have to go through so much with this man? How can you say you love someone and be so cruel to them? My mother always told me, "You never hurt or harm anything or anyone you really love." I would never treat a dog the way he treated me and my oldest son. Mick would use his feet to kick me out of the bed some nights. I would be so tired the next day. Who does that? A person with cruel intentions.

Little did he know men were after me, but I would refuse them because I wanted to do what was right. I have always lived by my Bible and what God has to say about the things in my life.

To anyone who's reading my story and going through similar things, *PLEASE* let someone know what is going on in your life!!! God always revealed things to me in visions, which always came true. I had to trust God. I had no one else to trust or believe in, and He always brought me through tough times.

Mick always provided for us with a roof over our heads and food on the table. He just wasn't nice to me and his children, and *that* is important to mention. There is no amount of provision that should cost you your mental, physical, and emotional health. I cannot remember even one day when life was good with him.

I can remember him pulling over on the dark road late one night to kick me out of the car because my sister and I were what they used to call, "jammed up and jelly tight."

He told me, "You cannot visit your family ever again."

I told him that he was crazy and that my family would always be here, even when he was gone.

When we arrived home, he tried to hit me but missed every time. I, in turn, pushed him, and he fell and hit his head on the corner of the table. I ran to the bedroom and locked myself in.

He kicked the door down, and I told him, "Don't hit me. I'm leaving."

He told me to get out of his house. I left and went to his uncle and aunt's house.

The first night, Mick's uncle called our house and asked to speak to me, and Mick lied and proceeded to tell him I was asleep. His uncle called to throw Mick off so that he wouldn't think that I was actually at their home. I cried and stayed with his aunt that night. The next day, he called me at work, begging me to come back home. The worst part is that I found out my oldest son remembers all of this. How sad is that? I was done.

I had had enough, so I threatened to divorce him. He bought a shotgun and threatened to kill all of us. I told my girlfriend, and she told me I needed to get out of there. She told me to make up anything to get out of the house that night, so I told him I was going to show her how to use and sell Mary Kay. He must have known that I was up to something; he hit the ceiling and tried to attack me. I grabbed up my kids and tried to run. He took my baby, ran into the room, and locked the door.

I cried out, "Give me my baby!"

If the baby had not started crying, there's no telling where we all would be today. I think in our graves, but by the grace of God and His mercy, we live.

I took my two sons and left running.

My oldest son said, "He's coming, Mommy. He's coming."

I said, "Run, baby. Run as fast as your little legs can carry you."

We made it to the car. I had just gotten a new five-speed stick and did not know how to put the car in reverse.

I prayed and asked the Lord, "Please, if it's in your power, put this car in reverse for me."

God showed me favor and did it, and we got away.

I took my kids to my parents' house, and that's where we resided until I was forced to move to California. Mick would stalk me and sometimes sneak up on me. No one knew what I had to endure until the end, when I started to expose the real person who I married. The night I left running, I never looked back on the marriage; to me, that was over. I would tell my mother I did not want myself nor my kids to end up a statistic.

My cousin in California told my mother I could bring the kids and come live with him and his family to start a new life. Before leaving for California, I filed for a divorce, and it was like a burden had been lifted off my shoulders. Mick did not contest the divorce. I found out a couple of weeks after leaving Mick that he had a child on the way with another woman. They had a beautiful little girl, whom I call my daughter to this day. I felt she had nothing to do with what her father and mother did to me. I had always wanted a little girl, but Mick said he didn't want any more kids. God knew best with what I was going through with the two boys.

I was kidnapped twice by Mick before leaving Florida. I ultimately needed to leave so as to not become a statistic. The first time was when I left him for the first time. Mick asked me to go somewhere with him to talk about our relationship. I agreed to go with him—that was a big mistake. He took me back to our old apartment and held me there until morning, then took me back to my mother's house.

I sat in a chair, all balled up, while he sat on the floor in front of me and said all kinds of unpleasant things to me. He had the audacity to ask me, "What did I do so bad that you would leave me and take our kids away from me?" *Really, Mick? Did you have to ask?* He knew exactly what the reasons were. I was so upset and afraid, remembering he had the shotgun in the closet. Thank God he never bought it out.

The second episode was when I left for good, and he asked to take me out to dinner. Like a fool, I agreed, not realizing the same thing could happen again—and it did. Back to the apartment, instead of dinner, to antagonize me. How could I be so stupid to fall for his lies again? Yes, I did let him talk me into going out with him, knowing our marriage was over. I managed to get through the torture and live another day.

I know you're asking, "Cheryl, how could you fall for the 'okey dokey' again?" Right! Well, I learned not to believe everything you hear—especially from Mick. He would never be able to con me into hearing him out in person ever again in this lifetime or another lifetime. I will only talk to him over the telephone, the only way he is allowed to converse with me.

In July 1985, the divorce was finalized, and we had joint custody of our two boys. Next was getting him to pay child support for the boys. I wanted nothing from Mick but my freedom. I told him I'd work three jobs just to take care of my sons, and that is what I did until my lawyer told me I was entitled to the money for my boys. I went after him for child support and won. Boy, was he upset and angry with me.

My life got better with Mick out of it. I went on to finish college with a number of talents underneath my belt to make a good life for my children. The advice I would leave with everyone is to put God first and trust Him, for He will bring you through whatever balls life throws your way. My motto is Philippians 4:11–13: "Not that I speak in respect of what: for I have learned, in whatever state I am, therewith to be content. I know both how to be abased, and I know how to abound: everywhere and in all things I am instructed both to be full and to be hungry, both to abound and to suffer need. I can do all things through Christ which strengtheneth me."

I can truly say that had it not been for God's grace and mercy on me, I would have never made it through my marriage with Mick. I relied on the word of God throughout my life and marriage, and guess what? Here I am, alive and free, because God has made me free. If I had it to do all over again, I would listen to that little, still voice that said, "Trust me, and do not marry this guy." My life would have been so much easier if I had listened and followed my first mind. Who knows where I would be, what I would be doing with my life right now, or who would be beside me had I obeyed that message.

Stay encouraged to wait on and listen to the Lord so as to not step out of God's will. Psalm 27:14 says, "Wait on the Lord; be of good courage, and He shall strengthen thine heart; wait, I say, on the Lord." This, too, is another Bible verse that I relied on and that kept me going. Psalms 27 is my favorite Bible verse. To whoever is reading my story, I pray that I have shared something that could be helpful to you.

I shared my story to let you know that trouble doesn't last; it can and will end at some point in your life. Isaiah 41:10 says, "Fear thou not, for I am with thee; be not dismayed, for I am thy God. I will strengthen thee; yea, I will help thee; I will uphold thee with the right hand of my righteousness." I can truly say my life has changed for the better after the life I shared with Mick. God allowed me to marry being unequally yoked.

I literally learned what it meant when my mother would say to me, "If you make your bed hard, you have to lie in it." I had to lie in it for six long years, and it taught me to be independent and trust God. My relationship with God became stronger. I got even closer to God and my family.

God asked me one day, "How do you expect to see me in Heaven hating your ex-husband? You must forgive him to get to me."

I had to go to Mick and ask for his forgiveness for whatever part I played in our marriage that led to our divorce.

Mick, to this day, has never apologized to me nor to my kids for what he did to our lives. He thinks he did nothing wrong and made no mistakes in our marriage that would lead me to divorce him. He said it "wasn't that bad." I don't hate him anymore; as a matter of fact, I had to take care of him after he had a stroke.

Mick was dating a younger woman at the time of his stroke; she left him, and his daughter, his sons, and I had to take care of this man. The only time this young lady came to see him is when she found out he had received a large amount of money. When the money was gone, so was the young lady. Mick never offered me nor his kids a penny. Of course, I did not want his money or anything from him because God supplies all of my needs and some of my wants.

Life is like that, but you get whatever seeds you sow in life, and I always try to sow good seeds, for I do not want my mistakes to come back on me or my kids. To this day, the kids still have to look out for their father. I am no longer involved in his life nor am I caring for him. He had a heart attack and three strokes but is still spending his life being mean to his children. I continue to pray for him and the things he faces in life. I made peace with him and myself a long time ago. Together, we have three children, ten grands, one great-grand, and one on the way. I can truly say God has been good to me and my family, and I thank Him each and every day.

I can remember the Tyler Perry movie, *Diary of a Mad Black Woman*, coming out. I could see myself in this movie, taking care of a man who abused me and cheated. Only by God's grace was I able to take care of this man. One would really have to humble himself under God's mighty hands to be able to tolerate this man being on his sick bed and still mean. The only good thing I could say about Mick is that he was a good provider as long as we were in his household.

I have not begun to tell all of my story about being married to this man, but I have given some important details for the most part. I have truly been bent but not broken. He tried to break me in many ways but was unsuccessful. I am still standing tall. I've had a lot of ups and downs in my lifetime, but being married to Mick was really the biggest challenge of them all. I now tell myself that if I can get through being married to Mick, I can get through anything I have to face from that day forth. "I can do all things through Christ who strengthens me." This, too, shall pass—and guess what? The problems always pass in due time. I am bent but not broken.

Cheryl Mutcherson

Chapter 11

ANCHORED: BECOMING THROUGH LIFE'S STORMS

This one is for my golden girls . . .

Nanny—thank you for going ahead and laying the blueprint for me and others. Your legacy shines brightly through us.

Mama—for blocking every obstacle and clearing every path put in front of me . . . #rydeordie

Parker—for reminding me daily of God's limitless favor and grace. Remember: You come from greatness, and you will be and do exceptional things because God said so . . .

— APC

I can still smell the fried chicken in the pan frying before even making it to the front door. I still feel the plastic sticking to the back of my legs on Nanny's elegant white couch with the antique legs. I will never forget the *All My Children* theme song blasting on the TV as Papi stood wiping the sweat falling from his face while standing over the stove.

"No, you cannot change the channel, Domonique. I'm watching the stories."

I cannot even count the number of times I was caught rolling my eyes, not understanding how he could possibly be watching the stories while cooking in the next room. I recall the solid oak dining room table with the floral plastic covering where we prayed and ate all our meals, crammed around the table too small for us all to fit, but so cozy and full of all my favorite foods, with echoes of laughter and hearts full of joy.

Most importantly, I'm remembering Nanny. Strong, regal, sharp, warm but stern. You could always find her sitting in her tan leather recliner—feet up, rocking back and forth with the cordless phone to her ear, having "church talk" with her girlfriends, her worn hands holding a Bible or something she was sewing. Her strong and commanding voice could startle the attention of a crowded room any day, but most days, she was yelling at my brothers: "Y'all better stop running in and out my house letting the air out!" To the world, she was Annale, a seamstress from Jacksonville, North Carolina who was sharp as a casket (as the elders would say) and loved the Lord, but to me, she was *everything*. She was my first anchor and God's most prolific show of favor in my life.

So many of the values and beliefs I hold dear, how I carry myself, and my deep-seated faith in God all stem from all of the lessons she gave and the seeds she was sowing in me for the first eighteen years of my life, unbeknownst to me. If only I knew then that stirring sweet potato pie mix *by hand* (Yes, she had an electric mixer . . . But let her tell it, it's better when you mix until "it feels done."), threading the needle, and/or practicing easter recitation speeches over and over again were lessons that cultivated values and beliefs that would shape me into the person I am today; I would have listened a little harder and asked a few more questions during that time instead of complaining or sulking. If only I had known . .

Now, they just sit with me like snippets from movie reels and talk to me like mantras or affirmations, faintly humming in my ear when I most need them.

"Keep God first."

"You will be the first . . ."

"Show up and show out."

"Put your head down and do the work."

"You're sharp. Use that brain."

Commonly, an anchor is a device, usually of metal, attached to a ship or boat by a cable and cast overboard to hold it in a particular place by means of a fluke that digs into the bottom of the ocean. In your faith journey, I view an anchor as something that grounds you firmly in your values and your beliefs; a constant reminder to keep a tight grasp on your faith, especially when there is turbulence around you. It could be the constant, pointing you toward the path

263

God ordained for your life, whispering quietly in your ear to be steadfast in your hopes and desires for the future.

Nowadays, I know God to be my anchor, but I won't ever forget Nanny being a mighty placeholder, preparing me, planting seeds, and priming me for the day when I needed to activate my own faith, own God's favor over my life, and create my own personal relationship with God. Today, I thank God for those prayers Nanny said for me and my family. We survived off of those prayers for a time.

If I had known then what I know now about how hard life can be, about all of the storms of life that would be thrown my way, and that I'd need to weather them without Nanny, I'd never have left the hospital that evening to attend a senior event with peers. I'd never left her side . . .

Friday, June 13, 2003

I focused on the sound of the rain pattering against the window as I blocked out sounds from my teacher and peers sitting in fifth period. I was gazing out the window, trying to fight this knot in the pit of my stomach. Something felt off, but I couldn't put my finger on it. *How could anything be wrong?* I thought to myself. *You're graduating from high school in days, and in weeks, you will be moving to Atlanta to attend your dream college—THE Clark Atlanta University.* No matter how much I tried, I couldn't shake the dark feeling casting a shadow on the most exciting moments happening right in front of me. Ten minutes later, the classroom phone rang. I jumped out of my foggy moment to my teacher informing me to head to the front office with my things. My heart sank.

As soon as I turned the corner to the front office and saw my parents, I knew she was gone. I locked eyes with my mom. Without words, her face said it all. She shook her head with fresh tears falling from her eyes, and I just remembered my legs giving out and feeling the warm, tight embraces from my parents. I couldn't stop the tears from falling down my face. *Why, God?* I wondered. I remember my tears matching the rain. I let my tears fall freely from Kennedy High to Platt Street. I distinctly remembered asking myself, *WWND? What would Nanny do?* I kept playing back what came to mind: Be strong. Be responsible. Pull it together. Accept God's will—He knows best. Be reliable.

I didn't cry again until the casket closed; at that moment, I knew I'd never see her beautiful dimples, feel her warm embrace, or hear her warm but stern advice.

"What am I supposed to do now?" my grandfather wailed. It shook me out of my own despair.

WWND? Be strong. Be responsible. Pull it together. Accept God's will— He knows best. Be reliable. Be there for others . . .

My anchor, my earthside center of gravity, had fought her good fight, finished her final assignment, and endured her final storm. I didn't know yet, but I was just experiencing my first. WWND quickly turned to WWJD *(What would Jesus do?)*.

I went on to experience many more storms as I navigated the complexities of being a young Black woman coming of age and traveling the road less traveled. I'd need to refer back to the lessons I learned from Nanny, my earthside anchor, many, many times as I worked to deepen my relationship with my true anchor in the midst of the storms of becoming. Every storm looked different and brought new unexpected challenges, but when the storm cleared, it always brought a rainbow of deep personal evolution and strength of character, a more solid anchoring in my faith in God, and immense FAVOR.

In this short chapter, I share a few more of these milestone moments or storms and some of the lessons I learned from them. It is my hope that by capturing these moments, I will encourage and be a bridge for you and others out there working toward anchoring themselves in God more deeply as they navigate life's storms, accepting and leaning into God's plan and profound favor for their lives.

> » **Lesson Learned**: Our ancestors came before us to pave the way and to help protect us and build a foundation for our faith and character. It is our responsibility to act on it, own it, and walk in it. It is my responsibility to fully realize and strive toward God's divine purpose and plan for our lives. One day, the ancestors will no longer be earthside, and we will need to rely on our Heavenly Father and Him alone.
> » **Mantra:** I depend on God and God alone.
> » **Evidence**: Psalm 62:5–8 — "I depend on God alone; I put my hope in Him. He alone protects and saves me; He is my defender, and I shall never be defeated. My

salvation and honor depend on God; He is my strong protector; He is my shelter. Trust in God at all times, my people."

The First . . .

"I don't even know why people go to college. You spend all of that money, and then you end up in debt. I wouldn't have chosen that. There are some jobs where people who haven't gone to college make just as much."

My heart jumped out of my chest. Time stood still. I was frozen in my space. That's how I'd describe the moment my mom abruptly rewrote the narrative I told myself about why I had made the choices I made in attending and graduating from college.

My mom and I were having a heated conversation about my brother. Often, my mom and I would have intense conversations about her expectations being lower for my brothers. She always used to tell me that every child is different, and I'd understand once I had kids. Logically, I understand where she was coming from, especially now that I'm an educator and have a daughter of my own, but it definitely was a heart-shattering moment of truth.

I'd seen completing college (which I did on time in four years with a GPA well above a 3.0 without my Nanny; in Atlanta, miles away from my family in Connecticut; and without anyone in my immediate family to rely on, navigating the college experience alone) as something I had to do for them. Silly me, carrying some invisible knapsack of expectations because I *thought* it was an expectation for me from others. As you can see, the people pleasing or considering what others would expect me to do continued . . .

My mom was fifteen when she met my father in 1982 at a high school basketball game. I guess you should cue the LL Cool J "Around the Way Girl" video to imagine my mom wearing gold hoops and my dad in Adidas and diamond chains. Imagine them falling in love, young and naive to the storms brewing around them. I came three years later when my mom was a high school senior with plans to study engineering at Devry in New Jersey. By this time, my dad had dropped out of high school and was taking care of his family and living a life in the streets. My mom would attempt to continue her plans, only to return when leaving me with my grandparents each semester became too hard, and my father would make some choices that would leave him to a period of time in and out of jail.

Through it all, my mom—and, eventually, my dad—would go on to do whatever it took through various jobs and business opportunities to provide for our family. I always had my physical needs and wants met, and they always supported me in everything I wanted to do. There was nothing I could want for that I didn't get. If I dig deep, I don't remember them ever telling me I had to go to college. They just made whatever I asked for happen. At the same time, I don't remember a time when going to college wasn't an option for me. I always knew I'd go. Maybe subconsciously, Nanny's words were embedded in my heart: "You will be the first."

My parents shaped a lot of values and beliefs I'm proud of, like loyalty, turning nothing into something, and the power of changing, but choosing college and the path that would lead certainly made me feel set apart from them, and this discussion with my mother was bringing that to a head for me.

It was at that moment that I realized that graduating college was *my* dream. I always thought it was also what my parents wanted. I saw it as something I had to do for them—to realize their own dreams deferred. I began realizing that it was *my* dream, a part of *my* purpose, a proof point of possibility for what could be possible for my brothers and others in my family coming after me. *Whoosh!* It was, and still is, hard sifting through what your ideas, wants, and desires are versus others' when you're a people pleaser. (Oh! Have I said that explicitly yet? If not: Hello! My name is Ashia, and I am a recovering people pleaser.)

This really became a motivator for me, and I later came to acknowledge it as a part of my mission and purpose in life. I live to disrupt expectations about what is possible, or people's perceptions of what is possible, and claim and take up space in places I deserve but people may not think I deserve. Much of my work is about showing up in the space, sitting at the uninvited table, and shaking the atmosphere into believing what is possible. Daily, I thank God for giving me that revelation and the favor to have access to opportunities to do just that. Getting the vision is one part; executing it is another.

They say, "The grass isn't always greener on the other side." Yes—I'd learn quickly that the road less traveled is full of sacrifice, isolation, and hurt as you heal from past things that could hold you back. Graduating college was cool, and it was an important milestone for me, but it also came with a dark cloud looming in the distance.

I didn't realize I'd be navigating being the first in my immediate family to get accepted, attend, and graduate—and how hard it would be. Neither of my parents, nor my paternal or maternal grandparents, had attended college. They were hardworking, blue-collar folks. I didn't come from a family with a lineage in college graduation; "Just keep your head down and work hard to provide for your family" is what I'd always heard. (*And, of course, there is some real value in the real-life experience wisdom they've given me that I will forever cherish.*)

I struggled with the outsider-insider dynamics of my professional and personal experiences. I felt like I didn't fit in any of the spaces I occupied at home, with friends, and at work.

There were many moments when I thought to myself, *Maybe my mom was right.* Very early on, I learned that everything up until this point was only a sprint, and graduating from college was when the real marathon began. Navigating the transition to adulthood as a first-generation college grad was rough.

In my inner circle of community, I was perceived as the one who was successful and had it all together. I was privileged and knew no real strife. Some even made accusations that I thought I was better because I went to college, and most people were proud and had incredibly high expectations for me and all that I'd accomplish. (Here we go with these expectations again . . . Real or an illusion?)

At work, I was the outspoken Black girl who graduated from a small HBCU with no formal education training, so I had to work ten times harder to prove I was worthy of being in the space while navigating my own internal impostor syndrome about my worth and capabilities to perform like everyone else with their prestigious PWI degrees. These folks were only "teaching" for a few years until they applied for law school. There was no plan B for me. This was it. I was broke and in debt, and I lacked some of the foundational learning I needed to be prepared to meet some of the demands of obtaining my teacher certifications.

To make matters worse, I couldn't speak to anyone—or I wouldn't let myself speak to anyone who could help me navigate this. I just kept thinking, *No one will understand, not even my parents.* Here I was again, telling myself not to fold: *Folks have these expectations. They expect you to SHOW UP. Be strong. Be responsible. Be pulled together. Accept God's will. Be reliable. Be there for others. SAVE FACE.*

My first year teaching ended in failure. After many failed attempts to pass my teacher certification test, I was unable to do so and needed to resign from my post. I remember calling in a favor to work back at my college job as a developmental services worker for the summer, afraid to share that I may need to stay past August, when the school year was slated to start. I was shattered.

I kept asking God, "Why, Lord? Bring me this far, and have it end in failure. What will I tell people? What will they think of me? How will I pay back these college debts?" It was hard, but in retrospect, staying where I was didn't align with His plan and my purpose.

I don't know why, but that entire summer, I kept reciting, "'For I know the plans I have for you,' declares the Lord, 'plans to prosper you and not to harm you, plans to give you hope and a future'" (Jeremiah 29:11). Slowly, my inner dialogue started to shift from what others would do or say, even Jesus, to what confirmation from God could anchor me right now. That became the scriptures. Now, I understood why learning the Bible and going to Sunday school were important. (Thank you, Nanny!) No longer were they words I could just recognize and recall; they had become embedded in my heart like an anchor, grounding and guiding my actions.

It gave me the energy and capacity to apply for other jobs in charter schools, where there was more flexibility with obtaining teacher certifications while working in schools. By August 1, I was teaching again at a high-performing charter school in my community. (Well, I started as a teacher assistant and was in that role for a short time. That's important to know.)

Have you ever seen that meme where you're crying because Jesus took your teddy bear, but behind His back, He has another one that's bigger and better? Well, I could have never imagined how that initial heartbreak was God setting the table for me to move into my purpose and His plan for my life. I would go on to have every role within the school, even sitting on the network team as a talent recruiter, all before becoming a principal in residence and, eventually, a principal within this organization all by the time I was thirty-three. Graduating college was only the beginning of being the "first" . . .

> » **Lesson Learned**: It is imperative to maintain trust in God when His plan for your life takes an unconventional path. That path may isolate you, and it may feel uncomfortable. (It's okay if you don't fit in every space you occupy.) It is a major part of God refining and sharpening your iron. Your detour is only a setup for your bright future. Press on.
> » **Mantra**: I trust the process. I do not let doubt or fear derail my faith or outlook on life. I am committed to believing that the best is yet to come.
> » **Evidence**: "'For I know the plans I have for you,'" declares the Lord, 'plans to prosper you and not to harm you, plans to give you hope and a future'" (Jeremiah 29:11).

"Trust in the Lord with all your heart, and do not lean on your own understanding. In all your ways acknowledge Him, and He will make straight paths" (Proverbs 3:5–6).

Principal Parks

Jesus was crucified in his thirty-third year. He spent the three years up until that point doing some of His most important work. Jesus changed the world that year. He saved humanity. It is because of this that some folks believe that age thirty-three is important—sacred, even. We all know that no one can measure up to the ultimate sacrifice Jesus made so that we may have access to God, but I surely felt that everything that had gone on up until this point was all for a purpose, and it was.

In March of 2018, I was selected as the principal of a founding middle school in Providence, Rhode Island. This Black girl from the Brass City, first-generation, with no formal education training, was given the privilege of making an impact at this level mere months after my thirty-third birthday. Talk about disrupting and claiming a seat at the table . . .

But we all know to whom much is given, much is required. While I knew that leading a school in a district where the state had taken over and the parents had fought for an alternative option would put our efforts under a microscope, this was, by far, one of the most important things I would ever commit to and embark on. It couldn't be that bad, right? I waited my whole life for this moment.

I always wanted to be a school principal. I remember playing in the basement of my grandparents' home with my friends and cousins. I was Ms. Natalie Woods back then. (Don't ask me why I loved that name, but I did.)

Mostly, I loved the role. I loved the relationships I cultivated with students and families. I loved the work of pouring into the culture. I loved having the agency to build systems and structures for a growing school. I loved coaching leaders and teachers. I loved creating a community, a family committed to supporting and empowering our students to be their best selves and exceed their goals and the very low expectations of others around them. I was committed to creating a space where my students could also be proof points. Maybe they'd be the first, too.

On the other hand, I was tired even before I started the role. I was running on autopilot, putting a decade's worth of subconscious pressure on myself to attach my worth and my identity into my work and to hustle so hard I'd never know poverty or be broke again. Or fail at work.

The work demanded a side of me that increasingly became unhealthy. I was at my prime of putting others before my own personal health and well-being. I set myself on fire constantly. I went to work when I was mentally and physically unwell. I even modeled that behavior for my leaders.

But they need me, I would tell myself. Who did I think I was? A martyr? Superwoman? Jesus? Your internal dialogue gotta be tight because if that self-talk isn't productive . . .

Who is going to break up the altercation between the students? Who is going to have that difficult conversation with the family of the student being retained? Who is going to real-time coach that leader in the class that is exploding with misbehavior? Well, if I am not there, could another student actually succeed at jumping out of the window of the second floor? I couldn't stop it.

Let's also talk about the fact that I didn't ask for help. Why didn't I ask for help? Impostor syndrome? *I'm not even supposed to be here. Will they think I am not qualified or fit to do the job because it is hard and taking a toll on me?* Every time I thought about it, my perceptions of others' expectations of me stopped me.

What happens when you get the thing you've always been praying for and realize it wasn't what you expected it would be? What happens when the tunnel vision, the grind to the seat at the table, is costing you everything? At this point, I missed my family deeply. I'd missed out on so many opportunities, experiences, and milestones with my friends and family. I was too tired on Sundays to even go to church. Above all, my relationship with my then-fiancé (HE'S MY HUSBAND NOW, y'all!) was suffering, and the disputes about me prioritizing myself and my health were constant. I was NOT *present* in life outside of work. I had no time or energy for it. I was on autopilot for two years.

God will deploy a forcing mechanism if needed. The beginning of my awakening, as I affectionately refer to it, was COVID shutting schools down. School closed for a few days, and I created and launched a remote school within a weekend. It wasn't until I was no longer in that environment in the same way that I had to sit with how unwell I was. How I had defaulted to work over self. How I had neglected my health, adopted unhealthy eating habits, and drank far too much alcohol after work each day. How outside of running laps around the school building, I had yet to work out or practice any physical activity. Sis was tired.

Something was tugging at me that I was out of sync and in misalignment with God. I listened to that voice, and it led me and my husband back to Connecticut. I thought if I got back to my anchor (my family and my old school community as the principal), I would be better. Do you think it got better? No—it got worse.

I treated the symptom as the root cause. Again, I was back to my old patterns of anchoring in all of the wrong things (people pleasing, living up to others' expectations, holding space for others' emotional energy and wellness versus my own, martyring).

I still had not addressed why I had set myself on fire and why my worth was connected solely to what I did for others. This year wasn't much different from past years. The only difference is that I learned I was pregnant. This news changed everything.

Early on in my pregnancy, I started bleeding for no apparent reason. This rocked my world. My husband and I went to the hospital, truly mortified. I wouldn't be able to live with myself if I, in any way, was responsible for us losing our baby. My husband and I had already lost a baby in the past, and it was certainly a sensitive spot for us. I just remember us praying so hard. Ultimately, I was okay, but given my age and medical history, my doctor was very direct about me needing to prioritize myself and health if I wanted to carry to full term. I had to make a decision and contend with my instinct to choose others over myself and, in this case, my baby. I worked from home the rest of the academic year, and then I resigned, and I haven't looked back.

Prioritizing myself and my family was, and still is, the best decision I have ever made.

A lot happened during that time to get to that place. The path was not linear. There were a lot of bumps and bruises, lots of twists and turns, a lot of stopping and starting over. But I've learned to extend myself grace. I've learned that God will never leave me nor forsake me; that His favor is limitless. He doesn't take it and then give it back, despite the choices we make. He's ten steps down the road, clearing a way or path and allowing the storms to happen so that our worth and our purpose is in alignment with and connected to His plan for our lives.

I know there is more to come, and until then, I'm clothed in His favor and anchored in His promises. I am fully present and full of gratitude for this journey so far. I am smelling the roses grown from the seeds planted many seasons ago as He prepares a place for me in the seasons to come. I know He's gonna "SHOW UP AND SHOW OUT!" like Nanny would say, and I'm here for it.

» **Lesson Learned**: I am not what I do. I am more than just what I do for others. Perfectionism is not what makes me valuable to others. I cannot pour from an empty cup. I deserve rest so that I can show up and carry out my purpose in life. I can be strong and worthy without supporting everyone else's weight.

» **Mantra:** I am not defined by what I do. I am enough. God says my value is more precious than jewels, and my worth is far above rubies and pearls. Only what He thinks matters.

» **Evidence**: "Who can find a virtuous woman? For her price is far above rubies. A worthy woman who can find? For her price is far above rubies. An excellent woman (one who is spiritual, capable, intelligent, and virtuous), who is he who can find her? Her value is more precious

than jewels, and her worth is far above rubies or pearls."
— Proverbs 31:10

"For You created my inmost being; You knit me together in my mother's womb. I praise You because I am fearfully and wonderfully made; Your works are wonderful, I know that full well." — Psalm 139:13–14

Ashia Parks-Coggins

Chapter 12

I LISTENED

I am very proud. I cannot believe of all the blessings that I have experienced in my life in the last three years. Could it be because I finally gained the confidence to try something new and believe in myself? All I can say is that I'm so happy I listened to Chandler and Aspen (A & C).

This chapter would not be possible without my amazing A & C. You gave Mommy the courage and battery to make it happen.

Phenomenal is such a powerful word. *Favor*, to me, means approval from God. God has shown me favor throughout my life, especially by blessing me with two extraordinary children. I can finally say that I am worthy of it all. But why the hell did it take so long?

What defines your favor? Is it the way you were brought into this world? Or do your actions make that decision?

Communication Through Community

As I think about my children, I am led to reflect on my own childhood. Growing up, I saw the world very differently. I watched my mother raise three children alone—alone in the sense of being married but having to bear the responsibilities as though she were single. I also saw my mother work two jobs and attend school to finish her nursing degree, while taking care of the three of us. I saw a strong woman.

As I reminisce about my childhood, I never considered how I was raised and if my specific childhood looked different than any other kid's. What I do recall was my experience while in school. I remember desiring the opportunity for my mother to visit my school for a function or event that was taking place. My mother was providing for us, and she did not have the flexibility to attend school functions like I wanted her to. I did not fully understand that back then, but now, as an adult—and as a mother—I get it.

I grew up in a large family household. We were a joint family; I grew up with four brothers and one sister. There was never a boring day that went by in our household. We were the Black Brady Bunch.

Looking back on my upbringing, I am grateful for all the crazy experiences my siblings and I went through. If I shared stories about all the crazy days that we had, specifically in high school, they would take up my entire chapter. As a teenager, I was clueless about my future. I can even say I was clueless as a young adult. I smartened up eventually.

Let's take it back to the good days when I didn't have a care in the world. I grew up in a unique way. In my opinion, I didn't experience or see a loving home that included both parents. I saw a single mom working two jobs to take care of her children while my dad was in and out of jail. I never experienced the daddy-daughter dances.

My relationship with my dad wasn't like the daddy-daughter relationships that you see on TV. That just wasn't my life. I will say, though, that there were other father figures in my life, so I never felt alone or left out. It was just my siblings and I being kids in the crazy world of New York City.

As a child, I believed none of this really mattered. However, as an adult, I now know that *all* of this did, indeed, matter to me. It impacted me throughout my life, and with God's favor and guidance, I was able to overcome those unresolved childhood issues.

When I was twelve years old, my mother remarried. I was then in a blended family, which consisted of six kids. For a moment, I thought I would finally get a loving home with two parents this time. I wanted to witness love. Unfortunately, I don't recall hearing "I love you" offered as endearing reassurance. It's not that we were not loved—we were. The act of communicating love was not a normal practice in our household or even in my extended family.

Many of the friends I went to school with had one-parent households initially, and we all wanted the same thing. I found this to be pretty interesting as a millennial, and my peers and I have had several conversations about the lack of love expressed and the general lack of communication present in the household as children. We all yearned to hear and feel love from our parents and/or caregivers.

Now, as millennial adults, we are attempting to properly demonstrate and communicate love within our own homes and with our children. It's like the old saying, "When you know better, you do better." I know that there are better, more effective ways to communicate love in my household, and I am practicing them daily.

My husband and I utter the words, "I love you," to our children. We hug and kiss them. We've taken the guessing game out of the picture; it's important to us that we are an example of love for them, that they feel and know that they are loved beyond doubt. Unlike me, they will have an example of a loving household and will be able to easily recreate their experience in their own homes when the time comes.

When I think about the familial communication that most commonly took place during my childhood, I think of statements like, "This is happening because of that," and "We aren't going here because of this." I don't have many memories of how we communicated as a family. We were so busy just being kids, really not analyzing our childhood and what we had or didn't have. This was in New York City prior to going to high school.

As a child, I also don't recall sharing my opinion with my parents or if it was even allowed. What I did know was that I needed to be able to take care of myself and be independent. I remember my mom telling me to always have my own and not to depend on anyone. I constantly heard that as a child, and it stuck with me.

What I Know Now:

- » Communication is always powerful.
- » Unresolved childhood issues have to be addressed and resolved.
- » Resolution will look different from person to person. Some may seek scriptures, and others will seek therapy. Find out what works best for you.
- » When you know better, do better. You can change family habits by creating healthy habits within your own family.

Favor

As a young adult, I didn't seek favor. I somewhat wanted a great job and nice things to have as my own. Unfortunately, I didn't see a crystal clear path to get them. When it came to relationships, I don't believe I sought God's guidance in my decision-making. How could I? I wasn't sure if I was Muslim, Catholic, or Christian, and I had no idea what book to follow for guidance.

What I did know was my ability to provide for myself and for my family. Remember: As a child, I saw my mother providing; thus, I, too, wanted to ensure that I always had my own, not depending on anyone.

The ultimate goal was to get a job that I actually enjoyed and make the golden number of six figures. *How can I get that? Do I have to know the right people?* The voice in my head always wondered.

What Determines a Career?

When I hear the word *career*, I'm somewhat taken aback, attempting to determine exactly what it means and to whom. After the age of eighteen, when landing a job, the focus was to specifically get a job that would turn into a career. I can admit that I spent way too many years at one company, believing that eventually, career progression would come with promotions and networking. That was a joke and tons of unnecessary politics, to say the least.

It wasn't until I got the courage to leave a job I was in for around ten years to realize that a career is what you make it. It can be a devoted passion project that turns into a business, or it can simply be something you enjoy doing in your downtime that brings you compensation and provides a good quality of life. As I started to research the different job opportunities that provided more resources and a work-life balance, my perspective seemed to shift.

I began to identify ways to update my resume. I also started to meet people who were in positions that, in my eyes, allowed flexibility and financial stability. That's when I realized that it's important not to be the smartest person in the room.

At the age of forty years, I finally gained the confidence in myself to believe that I deserve nothing but the best. I finally had a job that compensated me to my golden number, and I was actually learning to enhance my skills personally and professionally. It happened for me: I felt God's favor.

He favored me because I trusted Him. I listened to the voice that told me to leave a job I'd been comfortable in for ten years. I listened to the voice that told me I was worth more. I could do more, and I could earn more.

What I Know Now:

» Trusting God is difficult at times but rewarding all the time.

» God's favor is looking for us, even when we're not looking for it. I didn't know what spiritual practice I subscribed to initially, and God still favored me.

» Favor is not something that you can earn. None of us "deserve" it. It is given as an act of God's love for each of us.

» Obedience is better than sacrifice. Listening to your inner voice, to God, will save you from heartache and pain.

» Dreams do come true. I wanted to make six figures, and I positioned myself to achieve that dream by submitting my will to God's will.

That Mommy Joy

I remember when I first became a mom. It was one of the best feelings in the entire world. I remember saying that I was not going to have any children—now, I cannot imagine my life without my children. Becoming a mom is one of the best things that has ever happened to me, and I feel as though being a mother is a destined gift of mine. My two children are badasses. When I say they are badasses, I am saying that they are confident, they are kind, and they are smart as hell.

I can't believe that they asked me to help them write books when they were toddlers. I cannot believe that I listened to two toddlers who wanted to write books and actually paid thousands of dollars to get them published. There is no way in hell my family would have paid for any of us to publish a book growing up. Times are very different, and I am grateful for that.

When my children were young, I made it a priority to nurse them as long as I could. That was one of the hardest jobs I've ever had. I remember drinking gallons of water every day to ensure that they had enough milk to drink with the best nourishment possible. I have never done anything consistently every single day for two years in my life for the betterment of another person. *Wow. Holy shit—that is phenomenal!* I guess I am not surprised that they are the reason that I am a business owner—in fact, I am a business owner with my two kids, who are now six years old and nine years old.

We have been in business for over three years now. We are in business because of their love for books. We are also in business due to an amazing mentor and sister, who gave me the encouragement to step out on faith. There was favor within her when I was very insecure about taking the business to the next level and helping other people. It was her words that gave me the encouragement to do the unthinkable.

Why did I not think that I was worthy enough to have my own business and leave my nine-to-five job, all while having an amazing marriage and being successful? It is amazing how blessings come into your life without you realizing it until they slap you in the face. My goal is to ensure my children don't carry the same self-doubt that I grew up with.

What I Know Now:

» Children can be a great source of inspiration. They are not jaded, and they sometimes see the potential that adults can miss.

» "A child will lead them" has been my personal testimony. I am grateful that my children's love for books has turned into a successful family business.

» Let's normalize listening to children. Hear them out because they are brilliant.

» Be the change you want to see in the world of your children. As you consider your childhood, make positive changes that empower your children.

» Do something that pleases the inner child within you ... and do it often. It will keep you youthful.

The Wife Life

I've been a wife for eleven years. That seems like a long time ... and maybe it is. There was no playbook for being a wife. When I think about marriage and what I saw growing up, I saw forgiveness in the married couples within my family. Forgiveness from pain. Forgiveness from infidelity.

Should I expect this because I saw it growing up? Do my childhood experiences impact my future? How can I be a better wife? These are all questions that I've asked myself over the years.

The Bible says a man who finds a wife finds a good thing. I'm a damn good thing! However, I want to ensure that I am truly demonstrating "a good thing." It's easy to simply be comfortable in marriage. I want the best for myself, for my husband, and for my children as they bear witness to our roles within our marriage.

Taking a look at myself and my interactions, I desire to be more loving and affectionate. I desire to laugh uncontrollably and live life unapologetically. I recently determined that maybe my desires are a direct response to my childhood, as I didn't grow up in an environment where affection was shared openly. I'm not an affectionate person. It could be because I grew up in a house with four boys. I saw how they curved the girls. I always thought it was pathetic to see girls being so aggressive with my brothers; to me, it stood as an example of how not to be when it came to relationships.

Now, as a wife and mom, I am making a conscious effort to be intentional in showing my love. My husband should feel loved. My children should feel loved. Hell, everyone deserves love . . . Since I am not quite sure if love is determined by actions or words, I give both.

I give the kids hugs and kisses. I listen to them and consider their thoughts and perspectives. I teach them, and treat them with, respect and kindness. I support them in their interests. I do as much as I can in the areas that I can. To me, this is love. I show up with this same energy for my husband.

What I Know Now:

» Love languages matter, and not only knowing your husband's love language but also *loving* him in his love language adds a tremendous amount of value to your marriage.

» When marriage isn't picture-perfect, change how you are looking at the picture. You may not be able to control anyone or anything else, but you can control your perspective and how much you pray.

» It's important to know how your husband wants to receive love.

» There are other examples of a successful "wife life" available, even if you were not raised in a home where you witnessed it.

» For my sisters who strive to be married, be "a good thing" while you wait. The Bible says a man who finds a wife finds a good thing, and he is out there looking for you!

Here's an Earful

To be honest, I still don't ask for help. There is no reason why, at the age of forty-two, I still do not ask for help. It's sad to admit this. As a result, I experience burnout and exhaustion. My ultimate goal is to be the best wife and mom I can be. However, I sometimes have a very hard time accomplishing that.

As I walk on this path of phenomenal favor, it's important that I'm transparent about what I struggle with and what I'm excelling in. I have learned and grown professionally, but I am still working on growing emotionally and financially. There are still insecurities within myself that I have to remove and overcome in order to truly believe that I am a badass and fully capable of being amazing in all areas of my life.

Sometimes, I feel like I have no answers, and that is where therapy comes in. Therapy can be very beneficial, and I am now learning to use services that can help me cope with various trauma, insecurities, and feelings of self-doubt. Confiding in my therapist has healed me from things I did not know were holding me back in life. As I've discovered my pain points, I've found new ways to allow healing to happen. I've opened my mind and liberated myself *from* myself. I am more gentle with myself, and that has created a ripple effect.

Feelings of self-doubt can be seen by your children; children see when you are in pain. They see you when you're having a great day. They also see you when you're extremely stressed out, and they also see you when you are very happy. They are watching—especially when you think they are not.

All I want my children to see is love all the time, and therapy has helped me with accomplishing that. I also want them to be able to experience tough situations and learn from them as they get older in order to be able to handle this thing called life. It's okay to be sad and hurt. Therapy has helped me develop emotional maturity, which has greatly benefited me and my family.

I am still working on identifying and getting to know myself and what is important to me. I am learning better ways to communicate with my spouse. I desire to have a lasting, "I love you" marriage that lasts until eternity. I also desire to be a positive example to my children of what love looks and feels like, which I actively work toward whenever possible.

Ultimately, I am still learning to listen. I am learning to listen more to my inner voice. I am learning to listen to the wisdom of those who share their experiences with me. I am still learning to listen to my husband. Most importantly, I am listening to God.

What I Know Now:

» Listen to yourself: You have the answers within you already. Sit with yourself by meditating or spending time in nature. Listen closely.

» Listen to your spouse: Your spouse knows a great deal about you and can be an excellent resource. Listen to your spouse to hear their wants and needs.

» Marriage is a two-way street. You will have to do your part to contribute to the success of it.

» Listen to your children: Children have a lot to say. Find the time to really hear their hearts. This will strengthen your relationship with them and allow them to feel heard and loved.

» Listen to God: Spend time with God to protect your sanity, sis! None of this stuff is in our control, anyway. The faster you learn to give it all to God, the better off you will be. Listen for His still voice speaking to you directly and through others he sends as His messengers.

Times will be scary and uncertain, but unexpected favor, obedience, and trust in God is what will give us the peace and prosperity we need to succeed.

I'm rooting for you, and I love you.

Listen, listen, and listen again.

Amyira King

Made in the USA
Middletown, DE
03 October 2023

40060174R00170